P

MAY 2015

CARING ECONOMICS

CARING
ECONOMICS

Conversations on Altruism and Compassion,

Between Scientists, Economists,

and the Dalai Lama

With a Foreword by **His Holiness the Dalai Lama**

Edited by Tania Singer and Matthieu Ricard

PICADOR

New York

www.picadorusa.com

www.twitter.com/picadorusa • www.facebook.com/picadorusa

picadorbookroom.tumblr.com

Picador® is a U.S. registered trademark and is used by St. Martin's Press under license from Pan Books Limited.

For book club information, please visit www.facebook.com/picadorbookclub or e-mail marketing@picadorusa.com.

Designed by Patrice Sheridan

The Library of Congress Cataloging-in-Publication Data is available upon request.

ISBN 978-1-250-06412-7 (hardcover)
ISBN 978-1-250-06416-5 (e-book)

Picador books may be purchased for educational, business, or promotional use. For information on bulk purchases, please contact the Macmillan Corporate and Premium Sales Department at 1-800-221-7945, extension 5442, or write to specialmarkets@macmillan.com.

First Edition: April 2015

10 9 8 7 6 5 4 3 2 1

Contents

Contents

Foreword

His Holiness the Dalai Lama

Today, we live in a truly interconnected world. In today's global economy, the destinies of peoples across nations, even continents, have become deeply intertwined. This unprecedented level of economic integration has brought prosperity to many and raised people's standard of living. However, there is no denying that it has also exacerbated the growing gap between rich and poor, not only between nations but also within nations themselves.

Concern about how to bridge this gap between rich and poor prompts many questions. Can something be done to make our economic systems fairer? Is the basic premise of our modern capitalist system—that the market's invisible hand will ensure self-sustaining efficiency—valid in today's globalized world? Is there any place for powerful positive human motivation, such as altruism, in our economic systems, or is the common assumption that selfish behavior reaps greater rewards correct? Is growth measured in terms of GDP (gross domestic product) really the best indicator of a nation's economic progress? Finally, and perhaps most important of all, we need to examine the connection between economic systems and our quest for happiness.

In April 2010, a group of people came together in Zurich, Switzerland, under the auspices of the Mind and Life Institute to discuss these and other questions over two days. The main question, "What is the relevance of pro-social motivation and altruism in competitive systems such as the dominant Western economic system?," took on added relevance in light of the 2008 global financial crisis. Participants included psychologists, contemplative scientists, and neuroscientists working on the foundations of economic decision making, cooperation, pro-social behavior, empathy, and compassion, and others working on innovative economic systems. I had the good fortune to be part of this stimulating conversation.

It became increasingly clear that fundamental rethinking needs to take place in the field of economics. Economics needs to broaden its horizons. Questions of fairness and more equitable distribution, as well as larger social and environmental impacts, need to be taken into account. There is a growing realization that ethics and compassion in economics are equally important; after all, economics involves human activity and the basic goal of promoting greater happiness and alleviating suffering.

I am happy to know that with the publication of this book, *Caring Economics*, the rich and thought-provoking exchanges that took place at the Zurich meeting can be shared with many other interested individuals. I am grateful to everyone whose contribution made the meeting and the book possible. The kind of economic system we should have is a question relevant not only to experts but also to each and every one of us. I look forward to the emergence of a new kind of economic system that combines the dynamism of the market with an explicit concern for more equitable distribution of its fruits. I hope that the discussions revealed in these pages will serve as a catalyst for bringing that about.

JUNE 27, 2014

Introduction

Toward a Caring Economics

Tania Singer, Matthieu Ricard, and
Diego Hangartner

These days whenever we turn on the television or pick up a newspaper, it seems that we are bombarded with discussions of an impending financial crisis and its possible remedies. Many of the proposed solutions do not address the depth of the problem but instead aim merely to resume business as usual. People increasingly recognize the shortcomings of such approaches, and the need to rethink our economic systems and actions on an individual and global level. For many, simply preventing another financial crisis is not enough. Around the world, young people and families, scholars and workers, activists and politicians are calling for a more caring, sustainable, equitable economy—one that does not accommodate the desires of a few elites but benefits the world's community through compassion and humanitarianism, and offers long-term care for future generations and the fate of the biosphere. Is such a system possible? What would it look like, and how could it change our world?

In April 2010, world-renowned scholars from such diverse

disciplines as economics, neuroscience, philosophy, contemplative practice, and business came together with His Holiness the Dalai Lama in Zurich, Switzerland, to investigate these questions at a conference entitled Altruism and Compassion in Economic Systems, organized and hosted by the Mind and Life Institute. The Mind and Life Institute emerged out of a series of interdisciplinary dialogues between His Holiness the Dalai Lama, scientists, philosophers, and contemplatives to investigate the mind and the nature of reality, and thereby promote well-being on the planet. Since 1987, these dialogues have explored a wide range of topics, from physics, cosmology, ecology, and ethics to destructive emotions and education.[1]

In many ways, Altruism and Compassion in Economic Systems was one of Mind and Life's most ambitious conferences, the vision of neuroscientist Tania Singer. In 2006, Tania joined a research program at the University of Zurich that brought together psychologists, neuroscientists, and economists to investigate the foundations of human pro-sociality and cooperation. By this time, microeconomists such as Ernst Fehr (later one of the conference speakers)[2] had already shown that people take fairness into account during economic exchanges; yet existing economic models were primarily based on selfish preferences. Concepts of compassion and altruistic motivation, which were frequently studied in psychology and were the focus of highly developed Buddhist practices, were still foreign to economic scholarship and the applied economic world. Tania wanted to bring these disciplines together to explore how competitive economic systems could be reconciled with humanitarian values and pro-social motivation. She proposed the idea to Mind and Life and joined forces with head of Mind and Life Europe Diego Hangartner and French-born author and Buddhist monk Matthieu Ricard, and planning for the conference began.

At first, some scholars questioned what Buddhist and contemplative studies could bring to a discussion of economics. The two sets of ideas seemed divergent—the former concerned with compassion, voluntary simplicity, and reducing suffering, the latter with the pursuit of material wealth and the external conditions of comfort and well-being. Yet these systems also have something important in common: they are both designed to foster human happiness. Have they delivered on their promises? Tania, Matthieu, and Diego wondered what would happen if these disciplines came together in conversation with neuroscience, philosophy, and business. Could the conference participants envision an economic system that delivered both material prosperity and human well-being? The dialogues that ensued provided insights into the nature of economic systems and actions, and offered a new model for *homo economicus* as a fundamentally pro-social being.

Toward a Caring Economy

*What we begin with is this premise: since what we seek is
happiness, the most valuable resources are those that lead to
this goal.*[3]

Many people assume that money and happiness are inextricably linked, rising and falling together. The more money we have and the more things we own, the happier we are. Likewise, if we have less money and fewer things, our happiness is diminished. To some extent, this is true. People who have escaped absolute poverty and can exercise some financial freedom show greater rates of happiness than those who are struggling to meet their basic needs. For a while, as income increases, so does happiness.[4]

But this increase slows, and then eventually stops. Incomes have risen dramatically around the world since the 1960s, but happiness levels have stagnated. This is partly due to social comparison. We tend to evaluate our individual success based on the relative income of our peers, so that increases in income across a group of people do not necessarily lead to a collective increase in happiness.[5] This might also be explained by a fundamental truth of Buddhism: that happiness based on outer conditions, whether our possessions, our bank account balance, or our social status, is always limited and deceptive.

Think about a time when you bought a new car or got a raise. How did it feel? Once a few weeks or months had passed, did that feeling of excitement and contentment remain? Probably not. The trouble is that instead of learning from this and seeking a deeper, more sustainable source of happiness, many of us get caught in a cycle of craving and dissatisfaction. Eventually more money does not create more happiness, but simply a desire for more money, the next car, a bigger raise. This cycle can produce greed, grasping, and sometimes even a willingness to harm others in order to fulfill our own self-centered interests.

Research by psychologist Tim Kasser has shown that people with primarily materialistic values lack empathy and are unhappier, have fewer friends, and are even in poorer health than those who grant greater importance to internal values.[6] Yet economic theory has long proposed that people are fundamentally self-interested, and thus that capitalist economies can only function by providing opportunities for people to advance their own desires. As Adam Smith said in his *Wealth of Nations*, "It is not from the benevolence of the butcher, the brewer, or the baker that we expect our dinner, but from their regard to their own interest. We address ourselves not to their humanity but to their self-love, and never talk to them of our own necessities, but of their advantages."[7] Likewise, one of the founders of neoclassic economic systems, Francis Edgeworth, wrote, "The first principle of Economics is that every agent is actuated only by self-interest."[8]

Luckily this is not the whole story. Recent research suggests that each of us possesses a great capacity—maybe even a biological proclivity—for compassion, cooperation, and altruism.[9] And unlike money, these internal resources can be generated without limit—"like love . . . they can be infinite."[10]

In order to develop and promote the practice of altruism, we need to understand clearly what it is and how it relates to human flourishing. As the conference participants discovered, this is not so easy to establish. Psychology and contemplative traditions such as Buddhism maintain that altruism is a motivation to act for the benefit of others. This allows for the possibility for a compassionate act to have a positive benefit on the actor as well. As long as the core intention is to help the other person and not oneself, it is still altruism.

By contrast, economists are primarily concerned with observed behavior, or action rather than motivation. Imagine someone makes a donation to a charity because it makes her feel like a good person. Perhaps all she's done is replace one kind of selfish action (for financial gain) with another kind of selfish action (for emotional gain). But according to behavioral economists and evolutionists, this is still altruism, since she incurred an economic cost and benefitted someone else—even if she did it to satisfy her own ego.

Imagine that Adam Smith's baker is altruistic. He sees that you are hungry and have no money. Wishing to alleviate your suffering and replace it with well-being, he gives you bread. Although the baker has lost some potential income in this transaction, he has gained something as well. When he sees you accept the bread, the reward center in his brain activates and he feels pleasure.[11] He has also benefited in that he has eliminated a cause of his own suffering, the painful experience of watching another person suffer.[12] If the baker gave the bread without expecting anything in return, his motivation is altruistic, even if he feels good about his action afterward. If he gave the bread to feel good about himself, to relieve his guilt, or to avoid criticism for his stinginess, his motivation is selfish. But in either case, a hungry person has been fed.

When confronted with another's suffering, some people might choose to simply leave so they no longer have to observe the upsetting situation. Others might give thinking that it could result in their own financial gain—or that they might be punished if they didn't.[13] Still others might be content to let help come from elsewhere. It seems that we are far more skillful in avoiding our own suffering than in relieving the suffering of others—even though the latter pays huge dividends.

So how do we create a system in which people directly and regularly contribute to the well-being of others? We are all embedded in social worlds that greatly affect our successes and failures, as well as our outlooks and decisions. When the global economy collapsed in 2008, it was not only selfish people who lost money and suffered, but charitable people too. In fact, the poorest suffered the most.[14] We can no longer afford to think of ourselves as insular beings. Our well-being is interdependent (a truth long espoused by Buddhist thought), and becoming ever more so as cultures, markets, and people around the world increasingly trade goods and ideas. As His Holiness the Dalai Lama said in Zurich, "I often tell people that we should eliminate the notion of 'they.' 'We' should be enough; the whole world is part of we. . . . Economically, at every level, we need them. I want happiness, so in order to fulfill that, I need you."[15]

The world is in need of a dramatic reorientation of our financial systems. We need to take into account the internal, social, and environmental costs of economic gain, and vice versa. Just as previous studies of contemplatives have revealed our ability to literally transform the neural pathways of our brains through mental training,[16] perhaps here too we can transcend our current systems and create a more holistic and caring economy.

For most of us, the answer is not to start giving everything away. We need to understand *how* to give—the motivations, circumstances, and practices that will make our giving as effective as possible. It won't be simple, but the research presented in this volume gives us cause for great hope. It tells us that altruism can be learned and cultivated, and that its rewards are profound. We believe we can transform our economic policies and actions into a force for good—a force that fulfills both short- and long-term aspirations for the protection of the environment, material prosperity, and meaningful, personal satisfaction for all.

Overview of the Chapters

This book recounts the discussions that took place at the Altruism and Compassion in Economic Systems conference in Zurich in April 2010. The transcripts have been edited for content and clarity, but the book remains a faithful representation of the events. The book is divided into three sections, offering scientific (part I, chapters 1–5) and Buddhist and economic (part II, chapters 6–10) perspectives on altruism, as well as examples of altruism in practice (part III, chapters 11–14). The conclusion offers a synthesis of these perspectives and gives us guidelines for the future.

Each chapter is based on an individual presentation from the conference. The chapters appear in largely the same order in which the presentations occurred. (One notable exception is that Tania Singer's two presentations have been combined here to form chapter 2.) Each presenter first described his or her research and initiatives, and then opened the table for discussion with fellow panelists. As at many conferences, the presentations (and tea breaks!) occasionally went long, so some sessions allowed more time for discussion than others.

His Holiness the Dalai Lama and his longtime English translator Thupten Jinpa participated in every session. His Holiness can follow and articulate complex scientific and philosophical arguments in English, but he sometimes chooses to speak in Tibetan. In those cases during the conference, Jinpa would then translate what His Holiness said into English. In this book we have represented the translated speech as His Holiness's own words, without noting Jinpa's role except where he contributes to the discussion from his own perspective. During the conference, other presenters occasionally used a Tibetan word or phrase to describe a particular phenomenon. The Tibetan is rendered phonetically in the text with Wylie transliteration in an accompanying endnote.

In chapter 1, Dan Batson explores the egoism-altruism debate, asking whether human beings are ever motivated by something other than self-interest. In chapter 2, Tania Singer reviews neural research into empathy, compassion, and other motivational systems in humans, questioning the extent to which we can self-regulate these powerful emotions. In chapter 3, Richard Davidson presents data on the differences in pro-social behavior among children, expert practitioners in compassion meditation, and individuals who have undergone compassion training. In chapter 4, Matthieu Ricard provides a basic Buddhist understanding of altruism and discusses its possible applications in secular realms such as nursing. Joan Silk rounds out part I in chapter 5 by discussing instances of altruism in primates whose motivating factors may not, in fact, be entirely altruistic.

In chapter 6, Ernst Fehr describes the social dilemma experiment, which simultaneously tracks people's trust in altruism and real altruism, and introduces the idea of altruistic sanctioning. In chapter 7, John Dunne speaks from a Buddhist perspective, arguing that true happiness is based on internal resources that can be cultivated limitlessly. In chapter 8, Richard Layard questions whether economic growth always leads to increases in happiness. In chapter 9, Bill Harbaugh reviews research on the economic costs and psychological benefits of charitable giving. He proposes "warm-glow altruism" as an important alternate motive for giving. In chapter 10, Ernst Fehr steps back to ask why altruism matters and how it can solve social problems. He relates this to the creation of public goods and their role in equitable societies.

In chapter 11, Antoinette Hunziker-Ebneter demonstrates that smart investment can generate social, environmental, and financial profits at the same time. In chapter 12, Arthur Vayloyan describes a pioneering microfinance program that connects the wealthy with the poor to help people lift themselves out of poverty. In chapter 13, Bunker Roy describes the Barefoot College, an alternate educational system that rejects elitist understandings of knowledge to value folk and rural wisdom. In chapter 14, Bill George discusses the qualities of true leaders—how they are discovered and fostered, what we expect of them, and whose interests they serve.

In the conclusion, Joan Halifax joins with other presenters to recap the previous days' discussions and address questions that arose during the events, including the role of gender and intelligence in altruism. His Holiness acknowledges the many hopeful signs of progress, and reminds us of the ultimate importance of fostering secular ethics. Together, the chapters paint a surprising picture of the latent possibilities to forever transform the way we think about markets, communities, and our human potential for compassion, empathy, and happiness.

Many advances have occurred in the burgeoning field of neuroeconomics in the last three years. Several conference speakers—including Richie Davidson, Richard Layard, Ernst Fehr, Bill George, Bunker Roy, Joan Halifax, Matthieu Ricard, and Tania Singer—have been invited to participate in symposia such as the World Economic Forum and the Global Economic Symposium. Other participants have collaborated on projects to increase global happiness (Richard

Layard); and to bring solar electricity, rainwater harvesting, health, and educational initiatives to Himalayan and Indian communities (His Holiness the Dalai Lama, Bunker Roy, and Matthieu Ricard). Dan Batson and Matthieu Ricard have also collaborated on additional research and writings on altruism. These are just a few of the numerous initiatives that have been undertaken by people who met for the first time or were newly inspired at this wonderful event.

It was our privilege to be part of this groundbreaking symposium in Zurich, and it is with equal pleasure that we now present this book. We hope it will serve as an inspiration to readers, thinkers, and compassionate actors everywhere to participate in the creation of a pro-social economic system that benefits us all.

PART I

Scientific Research on Altruism and Pro-Social Behavior

1

The Egoism-Altruism Debate
A Psychological Perspective

Daniel Batson

Dan Batson, an experimental social psychologist, is a professor emeritus at the University of Kansas and the author of Altruism in Humans. *His research focuses on the existence of altruistic motivation, the behavioral consequences of religion, and the nature of moral emotions.*

Dan's presentation explored the egoism-altruism debate. He shed doubt on the common Western presumption that humans are always motivated by self-interest by providing experimental evidence that altruism does exist, and that it arises from feelings of empathic concern. In the ensuing discussion, the panelists compared Dan's research to Buddhist conceptions of how people can cultivate altruism, and the circumstances in which altruism may be extended to strangers and members of out-groups.

Your Holiness, I know that you are deeply convinced that altruism and compassion play a crucial role in human life, and that for many years you have cultivated these qualities through your spiritual practice; so it may come as a bit of a surprise to hear that in Western thought, particularly in psychology and economics, there is much doubt and debate about whether altruism and compassion even exist. There is a conviction that all human action, no matter how noble and seemingly selfless, is motivated by self-interest or egoism. The question is always, what's in it for me? As research psychologists, my colleagues and I have been trying to address this issue and see whether the Western view is correct.

I would like to begin by talking about the egoism-altruism debate. Let me explain what those terms mean. In this debate, *egoism* is a motivational state with the ultimate goal of increasing one's own welfare. That is contrasted with *altruism*, a motivational state with the ultimate goal of increasing another's welfare. What I mean by "ultimate goal" here is not a first and final cause, but what the person is truly after in the situation. That's different from an instrumental goal, which is something one pursues as a means to some other end. The reason this is an important distinction is that egoism and altruism can both motivate helping behavior and cooperation, even very costly helping. But egoism claims that all acts of kindness toward others have the ultimate goal of increasing one's own welfare. For example, one could be seeking to feel good about oneself, to feel a warm glow, or to avoid guilt.

The question then becomes, are humans actually capable of altruism? In Western thought, the dominant view is universal egoism. Here's a nice description of it from the Duke de La Rochefoucauld: "The most disinterested love is, after all, a kind of bargain in which the dear love of our own selves always proposes to be the gainer some way or other."[1] We're not just talking about material gains and punishments here; you could gain by avoiding social or self-punishment in the form of censure and guilt. The gains could also be social or self-rewards, such as getting praise from others or feeling good about yourself.

Another important possibility is that you help in order to reduce your own distress caused by witnessing another's suffering. That would still be an egoistic motive, because the goal is to benefit oneself. On that point the Dutch-born English philosopher and economist Bernard Mandeville made a rather extreme statement. He said, "There's no merit in saving an innocent babe ready to drop into the fire: The action is neither good nor bad, and what benefit soever the infant received, we only obliged ourselves; for to have seen it fall and not strove to hinder it, would have caused a pain, which self-preservation compelled us to prevent."[2]

Is this dominant egoistic view correct? That brings us to the empathy-altruism hypothesis. The hypothesis is that empathic concern produces altruistic motivation. This hypothesis is not original to me by any stretch; Charles Darwin, for example, proposed a version of it. A number of other people have also proposed this idea throughout history, but it's always been a minority view in Western thought. In this hypothesis, "empathic concern" refers to an other-oriented emotion evoked by seeing a person in need—a feeling *for* the person in need. It's not feeling *as* the person feels. Empathic concern includes feelings of sympathy, compassion, and tenderness for the other person. It's distinct from the feeling of personal distress I mentioned earlier—our pain at seeing the baby ready to fall—which is a self-oriented emotion.

Evidence has shown that empathic concern is associated with increased helpfulness. But this evidence, by itself, simply says empathy produces some motive; it doesn't say what the nature of the motive is. Is it an egoistic motive or an altruistic motive? When we help another person, we benefit the other, but we also receive self-benefits. The egoistic account is that the benefit to the other is simply instrumental; it's the means to the ultimate goal of benefiting ourselves. For example, an advocate of egoism might argue that when we feel empathic concern for someone who is suffering, we suffer too, and we are motivated to reduce our own suffering. It's just like personal distress in the sense that the motivation is to benefit ourselves, even if that motivation arises from empathic concern. That's an egoistic account.

The altruistic account is that benefitting the other is our ultimate goal. Our concern is for the other person's welfare. Yes, we benefit. We feel better about ourselves, perhaps we're happy that they feel better, and we avoid feeling guilt—but those are unintended consequences. They happen, but that's not why we act. We act because we want to help the other, not help ourselves. The research puzzle is how do we determine what a person's ultimate goal is in a given situation? You are acting to benefit the other, but is that an instrumental goal, or is that an ultimate goal?

To illustrate how my colleagues and I have tried to solve this puzzle, I'd like to briefly focus on one experimental procedure addressing the question of whether the motivation evoked by empathic concern is to relieve our own discomfort. In this particular experiment, female undergraduates individually observe another undergraduate, Elaine, perform a memory task. The observers do not know Elaine. Elaine's task involves trying to repeat back strings of digits to a research assistant. Elaine receives random electric shocks as she tries to remember the digits, ostensibly to study the effect of aversive conditions on the performance of such a task. (She does not actually receive shocks in this procedure. Participants are observing Elaine over closed-circuit TV, and what they're actually seeing is a videotape that we created for the experiment.) About halfway through the memory task, the assistant interrupts the procedure because it is clear that Elaine is finding the shocks very uncomfortable. Elaine explains that she may be finding the shocks so difficult because of a traumatic childhood experience when she fell off a horse onto an electrical fence. Elaine is in clear distress but says she will continue.

At this point, the observers are given a chance to help Elaine by taking her place—that is, do the memory task and receive the shocks. Half of them are told that if they don't take her place, they can just continue to observe her perform the task. We call this *difficult escape*. The other half are told that if they don't take her place, they will be free to go; Elaine will continue, but they will not have to watch. That's what we call *easy escape*. The idea behind this is that if participants are egoistically motivated to reduce their own empathic concern, then in the case of the difficult escape, they'll feel obliged to help, because that's the only way to turn off the stimulus that's causing their suffering. In the easy escape, they can simply leave, so they'll be much less likely to help Elaine. However, if empathic concern produces altruistic motivation, with the goal of relieving Elaine's suffering, participants feeling empathy should be just as likely to help when escape is easy as when it is difficult.

To test these competing predictions, we added another feature to the experiment. We assumed that watching Elaine react badly to the shocks would lead participants to feel a mixture of self-focused uneasiness and discomfort (personal distress) and other-focused warm, sympathetic feelings for Elaine (empathic concern). We induced half of the participants in each escape condition to misattribute their warm, sympathetic feelings to a drug they had taken as part of another experiment (actually a cornstarch placebo), and so they reported feeling predominantly personal distress as a result of watching Elaine. We induced the other half to misattribute their feelings of uneasiness and discomfort to the drug, and they reported feeling predominantly empathic concern.

What we found was that those participants for whom personal distress was dominant were much less likely to help if escape was easy than if it was difficult. That's the pattern we would expect if their motivation was egoistic, which seems to have been the case. What about the participants for whom empathic concern was dominant? For them, it made no difference whether they were given the easy or difficult escape option; a high percentage decided to help in both cases. (See figure 1.1.) This pattern is consistent with the empathy-altruism hypothesis. If your goal is to increase the other's welfare, leaving doesn't do that. The only way you can increase the other's welfare is by actually taking his or her place.

However, there are other egoistic explanations that could account for these data. For example, if the participants were motivated to avoid guilt, we would see this same pattern. But results of other experiments indicate that the motivation produced by empathic concern is not directed toward the ultimate goal of avoiding guilt. We've now conducted over thirty-five experiments to test various egoistic alternatives.

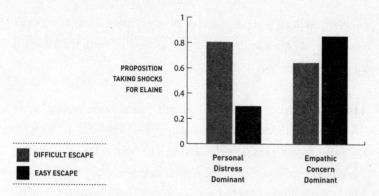

Figure 1.1: Participants induced to feel empathic concern for Elaine were very differently affected by the escape conditions than were those induced to feel personal distress. Those for whom personal distress was dominant were far less likely to help when escape was easy, indicating self-oriented egoistic motivation. But those for whom empathic concern was dominant were no less likely to help when escape was easy, indicating other-oriented altruistic motivation.

The results of these experiments have supported none of the egoistic alternatives that people have been able to propose; the data consistently support the empathy-altruism hypothesis. So our tentative conclusion is that the human motivational repertoire is not limited to egoism or self-interest. Empathic concern does indeed produce altruistic motivation, and this motivation is actually quite powerful. Thus I believe that we need to take empathy-induced altruism into account in our understanding of human behavior, even in economic systems.

What leads us to experience empathy-induced altruistic motivation? Two conditions seem to be key: valuing the other's welfare, and perceiving the other to be in need. I think the process begins with valuing the other's welfare. If you don't value the other's welfare, even if you perceive the other to be in need, it will not lead to empathic concern. But if you do, these two together will produce empathic concern, and that is what produces altruistic motivation, at least this form of it. My question is, how does this view relate to the Buddhist view of compassion?

Thupten Jinpa: There is a somewhat parallel understanding of the process of cultivating compassion in Buddhist practice as well. For example, one of the key elements that is required for experiencing compassion for someone is some form of appreciation of the other, which leads to some kind of connectedness with the other. And on that basis, a sense of the unbearableness of the sight of the other's suffering arises. Together these lead to compassion.

Dalai Lama: Usually when Buddhists describe other sentient beings, we refer to them as *mother sentient beings*. That means others are as dear to you as your own mother. So first we try to develop that kind of perception of others as dear.

Dan Batson: That relates to valuing others' welfare. Then, with perceiving the other in need, it should lead to empathic concern.

Thupten Jinpa: In the Buddhist understanding, the process would be first to cultivate the perception of others as dear and worthy of your concern. Then, when combined with the perception of others' needs, you cultivate the motivation to help others, which would then lead to actual altruistic behavior, or action.

Dan Batson: It sounds like we see the process in much the same way, although what I'm referring to as *altruism* is the motivation, which then would lead to the behavior.

Joan Halifax: Dan, does this hypothesis hold in relation only to someone who is from your in-group, like your family or your village, or also to a person who is stigmatized, or in an out-group, or in a nation that you are warring with?

Dan Batson: There has been research done on this, and certainly our tendency is to value the welfare of and feel more empathic concern for those who are near and dear. But it does seem that empathic concern can be evoked beyond the in-group, particularly if you can get people to focus and think about the suffering of others. We do that in the research; it's been done usually through what is called *perspective taking*, where you try to imagine what the other is feeling and how he or she is affected by the situation. I know the Buddhist contemplative tradition does it more through trying to think and discipline the thought, to automatically see the other as like mother, like child. But if you get people to take the perspective of the other, empathic concern seems to be evoked. We have found that we can do it for members of out-groups, stigmatized people, homeless individuals. It seems to be possible for anybody for whom you don't feel antipathy. That's where you lose the valuing of others' welfare, I think.

Dalai Lama: I always make clear that our discussion is simply on Buddhist science, and to some extent Buddhist concepts. These two things could be universal; the Buddhist religion is mostly for Buddhists. However, from a Buddhist practitioner's point of view, it's very important to discern whether or not your love, compassion, or sense of concern is based on attachment. As long as your sympathy or altruistic attitude is essentially based on attachment, then it is very limited. And that love or kindness or altruism based on attachment can easily change. Today, you feel concern. The next day, you wish harm and suffering on the other, because that is the nature of attachment. So for this practice you must first detach so there is no difference between an enemy and a friend. Your friends are sentient beings who want happiness and who also have a right to it. Your enemy also has the same right. So your sense of concern must be based on that understanding; that's the Buddhist way.

You mentioned that basic human nature is selfish. Now here, what is the exact meaning of *selfish* or *egoistic*? Egoism in a broad sense is just a feeling of "I." "I" is the center of the whole universe! That is present in all of us at all times. From the Buddhist viewpoint, even Buddha has that kind of egoism. Buddha naturally feels "I am." But that feeling of "I" has many levels. In order to practice altruism, we need a strong sense of self. This sense of self is the basis of willpower, the basis of enthusiasm, the basis of confidence. But on another level, with that "I" feeling comes attachment, and when attachment is there, hatred is also there. So some people, some sentient beings, form attachment to what they consider dear to them and useful to them. Attachment creates a feeling of closeness that brings a sense of concern, a kind of altruism. But because it's based on attachment, you cannot shift it toward your enemy, or to neutral people.

That belief, I think, is for Buddhists, not the general public. Other religions have parallel teachings. In theistic religions, the concept of a creator, as I understand it, has the same purpose: to develop faith toward God and to view all beings as created by God. All are from the same source, and you yourself have totally submitted to God. So that reduces negative egoism, and at the same time, when all others are created by the same source, there's no reason to make a distinction between "my friend" and "my enemy." If you go further, my enemy is also created by God.

Dan Batson: Let me just pick up on one thing that you said at the beginning there, which is that we all have egoistic motives, that is, self-interested motives. That's quite true. That's a helpful clarification here, I think, because the research demonstrating that we have altruistic motives is in no way demonstrating that we don't have self-interested motives. We certainly do, and in most situations both are operating. But we also need to recognize that altruistic motivation—that is, the capacity to care about the welfare of another—does seem to be within our nature.

Thupten Jinpa: To give an example, in the Buddhist context, one speaks of the highest form of an altruistic mental state, which is referred to as the *awakening mind*, or *bodhicitta*. Bodhicitta is characterized primarily by two aspirations. One is the aspiration to seek full awakening for the benefit of all beings, so that is other-centered, other-regarding. But along with it is also an aspiration to seek one's own enlightenment. So even there, there is recognition of the presence of self-interest.

2

Empathy and the Interoceptive Cortex

Tania Singer[1]

Neuroscientist Tania Singer has been a director of the Department of Social Neuroscience at the Max Planck Institute for Human Cognitive and Brain Sciences in Leipzig, Germany, since 2010. She investigates the neuronal, hormonal, and developmental foundations of human social cognition, emotion regulation capacities, and the role of motivation and emotion in social decision making. She also studies the effects of mental training and meditation on the brain and subjective and behavioral plasticity. Tania is on the board of the Mind and Life Institute.

Tania's presentation revealed the pathways underlying basic emotional and motivational systems as well as social emotions such as empathy and compassion. She showed how the human brain allows people to share feelings with others and mapped the neural routes underlying social behavior such as trust. Tania, His Holiness, Matthieu, and Jinpa discussed whether meditation can enable one to circumvent these biological processes.

I'd like to begin by defining some of the terms I will be using in my presentation, which focuses on neuroscientific research on social emotions and social behavior. For example, when we talk about phenomena such as empathy, compassion, and their sister states, we usually start with a phenomenon called *emotional contagion*. An example of emotional contagion is when a baby in a clinic starts crying, causing all the other children in the clinic to cry as well. It's as if you catch and share the emotions of someone else, remaining unaware that those emotions originated with another person. With emotional contagion, you lack a distinction between self and other, as in babies who cannot distinguish between their mothers and themselves. In order for empathy to arise, you need this self/other distinction. This distinction is at the center of the debate about whether animals have empathy and compassion, or whether they just display emotional contagion. If you have monkeys in cages and one makes a distress call, all the others will join in. But this does not necessarily mean that these monkeys have empathic concern or feelings of compassion; they may simply be experiencing emotional contagion.

I would like to define another important term: empathy. Empathy is the ability to vicariously share a feeling with someone else. You have pain; therefore I have pain. I am sharing a similar feeling to yours. But at the same time, I know that the pain I have is not mine; I know I am vicariously feeling your pain. Here, in contrast to emotional contagion, there is a clear distinction between self and other. This quality of sharing emotions or empathizing with others is not necessarily associated with pro-social motivation or behavior. Pro-social motivation requires concern and caring about the well-being of another person, and this in turn leads to pro-social behavior, or behavior that benefits the other.

Empathy can, but does not necessarily, lead to pro-social motivation and behavior.

For example, if I resonate too strongly with your pain and experience personal distress as a result, I will be preoccupied with reducing my own suffering and may even withdraw from you or be angry at you for affecting me so negatively. This would result in the opposite of pro-social motivation and behavior.

Here I want to make a distinction between empathy and compassion. In the case of compassion—what Dan Batson has also called *empathic concern*, and others call *sympathy*—you now have a real concern for the other. When confronted with the suffering of others, you do not necessarily share the same feeling but may instead have a feeling of warmth and love. Thus, you don't merely feel *as* someone feels (as with empathy); rather you feel *for* someone, and you have a motivation to alleviate their suffering. I think this is very close to the Buddhist notion of compassion, and this distinction between empathy and compassion is crucial. Empathy alone is not enough to create pro-social motivation and behavior; it needs to be transformed into compassion or empathic concern.

In social neuroscience we also make a distinction between the different neural routes that underlie our ability to understand the feelings and thoughts of others. Empathy and compassion rely on an affective neuronal route to the understanding of others. However, there is another brain circuitry system that subserves a more cognitive understanding of other people's thoughts and beliefs, which we call *cognitive perspective taking* or *Theory of Mind*. This is the ability to make cognitive inferences about the mental states of others.

Perhaps an example will clarify the difference. Psychopaths and certain kinds of criminals are very good at cognitive inference, even though they lack empathy. They know how to manipulate other people by gaining a good understanding of others' needs and intentions. What they lack, however, is empathic resonance with the suffering of others. In consequence, they display antisocial rather than pro-social behavior. This example illustrates how cognitive perspective taking and empathy can dissociate in psychopathology, and that these cognitive routes rely on different networks in the brain.

What I want to show you now is an example of how we measure empathy in neuroscience using brain-imaging techniques such as fMRI. In this experiment, we ask a couple to come into the scanner. Each partner receives bursts of intermittent pain through electrodes attached to their hands. Both of them can see a screen on which a flashing arrow signals which partner is currently receiving the pain stimulus. This allows us to measure brain responses when a person feels pain, and when a person feels no physical stimulus but knows his or her partner is suffering.

What we usually find in this experiment is that the neural network that underlies the processing of our own pain also gets activated when we know our partner is in pain. This network is in a region in the brain we call the *interoceptive cortex*, because it records everything that happens in the body and the resultant feelings. This part of the brain gets signals if, for example, your heartbeat or breathing pattern changes, and also if you become agitated because you are afraid or angry. This area is associated with all kinds of feeling states, including the sensations of pain and disgust. The interoceptive or insula cortex is crucial for processing your own feeling states, as well as processing what another person is feeling. Figure 2.2 illustrates how these two things are related.

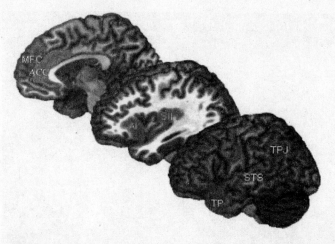

Brain regions activated in empathy for pain paradigms

Brain regions activated in Theory of Mind paradigms

Figure 2.1: The brain contains two different routes to understanding another person's mind and feelings. In this image, the main regions typically involved when empathizing with the suffering of others are ACC, AI, and SII. The main regions typically involved in Theory of Mind or cognitive perspective taking are TPJ, STS, TP, and MFC. MFC = medial prefrontal cortex; ACC = anterior cingulate cortex; AI = anterior insula; SII = secondary somatosensory cortex; TP = temporal poles; STS = superior temporal sulcus; TPJ = temporo-parietal junction.

If you see images of suffering faces, or if you see needles sticking in a hand, the same network fires as when you are processing your own pain, even if you are not conscious of it. These responses are automatic and very fast. This means we are all much more interconnected than we thought; we are representing the emotional states of others in our brains without even being aware of it.

The question is, if our brain is wired for such affective resonance and interconnectedness with other beings, why do we not

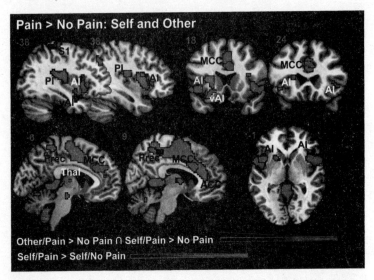

Figure 2.2A: This figure depicts the findings of meta-analyses on multiple fMRI studies focusing on the brain networks underlying empathy for pain.[2] The brain areas depicted in gray are activated when a subject is processing painful stimuli. The brain areas depicted in white are activated when the subject empathizes with another person receiving pain stimuli. Areas of common activation—that is, activated when the subject is in pain and when he or she experiences someone else's pain vicariously—include the anterior insula (AI), medial and anterior cingulate cortex (MCC/ACC), precuneus (Prec), and thalamus (Thal). Areas activated only during the personal experience of pain are the posterior insula (PI), primary somatosensory cortex (S1), and large parts of the medial and anterior cingulate cortex (MCC/ACC).

empathize all the time with everyone? What conditions can block empathic responses, or even reverse them, creating the opposite feeling of schadenfreude? Schadenfreude is a German word, but I think everyone knows the feeling. It is rejoicing in someone else's suffering instead of sharing in it. One place where we have observed schadenfreude is during experiments using monetary exchange

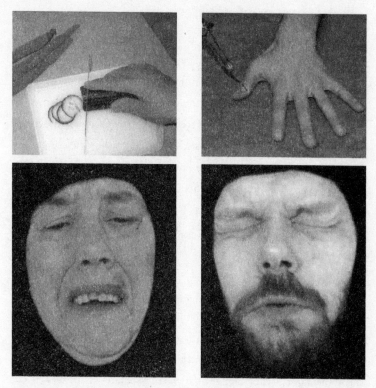

Figure 2.2B: Representative images meant to invoke empathy for pain. Here, we see two people grimacing from fear or pain, and strangers' hands being pierced and cut by a sharp object.

games conducted in the laboratory. We'll hear more about these games later, but basically what happens is that participants exchange money, and they can do so fairly or unfairly. After subjects played several rounds of the games, we measured participants' empathic brain response while they were watching fair and then unfair players receiving pain stimuli. This was similar to the empathy for pain experiment I explained before with the couples, but now we measured the brain responses of participants while witnessing a likeable, fair player receiving pain, and then their response to witnessing a dislikeable, unfair person receiving pain.

Men and women displayed different patterns of empathic brain responses in this experiment. Men showed an empathic response to the suffering of a person who played fairly. However, when observing an unfair person receiving pain stimuli, they showed a signal in a part of the brain, the nucleus accumbens, that is associated with feelings of reward and pleasure. (This part of the brain is also activated when you anticipate eating a piece of yummy chocolate.) We also gave questionnaires to the participants. The stronger the expressed need for revenge in the questionnaire, the stronger the reward signal was when the men saw the unfair person suffering.

In contrast, the female participants showed empathic brain responses when witnessing both the fair and unfair players experiencing pain. Even though their expressed dislike of the unfair players in the questionnaire was similar to the men's, they did not on average show the same strong signal of reward associated with feelings of schadenfreude and revenge.

We observed a similar modulation of the empathic brain signal in the interoceptive cortex in another experiment using in-group versus out-group perception. Here we measured the empathic brain responses of participants while they were watching someone whom they perceived as belonging to their in-group (a fan of their own football team) suffering as compared to someone who was part of the out-group (a fan of the rival team). The finding was that you have more empathy for people you perceive to be part of your in-group than for out-group members.

Thus empathy and schadenfreude represent essentially two

antagonistic motivational systems. If activity in one system is high, activity in the other is low. Furthermore, we showed that when empathy-related brain activation is high, you are more likely to help another person in pain. If, however, schadenfreude is high, you will refrain from helping. Thus, empathy brain signals in the interoceptive cortex predict helping behavior, and schadenfreude brain signals predict the absence of such pro-social behavior. In fact, the brain signal is a better predictor than what people say about whether they will or will not help. People are not always honest when it comes to admitting differential attitudes toward in- and out-group members.

These experiments also show that it is easy to switch from one motivational system to another, from empathy to schadenfreude. We should note that the subjects in all these experiments are generally nice, highly educated, healthy adults. All it takes is a slight change in instruction (leading to an in- or out-group perception of someone) or a previous experience (where you experienced someone to be fair or unfair) to cause you to switch from empathy to schadenfreude. The question, then, is how we can overcome this tendency to easily override empathy and whether the cultivation of compassion could alter this biological human disposition.

Another fact we learned from another series of experiments on empathy is that people who don't understand their own emotions and feeling states—we call them *alexithymic*—show a lack of activation in these empathy-related brain regions. To empathize with others, you first need to understand your own emotions and bodily states. Empathy training should therefore concentrate first on training people to recognize and understand their own bodily and emotional states.

After having spoken mostly about empathy research, I now want to show you some research that focuses on compassion. We think of empathy as a precursor of compassion. But can we measure brain responses associated with compassion isolated from empathy? Richie Davidson will talk more about this,[3] but basically we started working with long-term Buddhist practitioners to find out which areas of the brain are associated with the state of compassion and loving-kindness. We not only asked the practitioners to go in and out of this state, but we also asked them to regulate its intensity to 30, 60, or 100 percent, like when you cook and you can have a low, medium, or high flame. This may seem strange from a Buddhist teaching perspective, but for us it's very important to measure one's capacity to regulate emotion like a thermostat.

We observed that the interoceptive cortex and other areas involved in affiliation and reward are very strongly activated during states of loving-kindness and compassion, and we could also see the long-term practitioners nicely modulating this state and the underlying brain network, from 30 to 60 to 100 percent. We were astonished: what beautiful control of the mind!

Then we wanted to know, could we teach the cultivation of compassion and loving-kindness to naive people who hadn't been practicing in retreats for many years? Could we see changes in the brain—that is, gain evidence for brain plasticity in the networks associated with compassion—after only one week of training in people who had never done this before? And the good news is, there is hope! We conducted a series of different experiments with naive non-meditators. In our very first experiment, we investigated whether we could improve their ability to activate compassion-related brain networks through a new technique using real-time fMRI, where par-

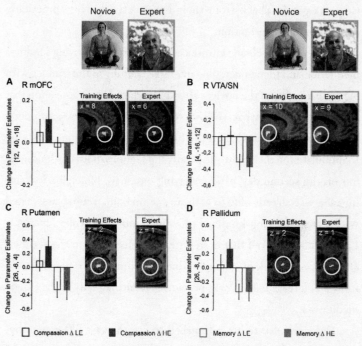

Figure 2.3: This figure depicts the effects of one-week compassion training on the brain. The control group was trained in memory techniques. These naive non-trained subjects were presented with highly emotional video clips depicting human suffering before and after the one-week training. After training, subjects who had undergone compassion training in comparison to subjects who had undergone memory training revealed higher activation in (a) the right medial orbitofrontal cortex (mOFC), (b) the right ventral tegmental area and substantia nigra (VTA/SN), (c) the right putamen, and (d) the right pallidum. These results are shown in the brain scans at left. The brain scans on the right show the neural activations of an expert practitioner elicited when he immersed himself in similar compassionate states.

ticipants got feedback from their brain activity while practicing loving-kindness meditation.

After one day of being introduced to and practicing loving-kindness meditation and then undergoing intensive training in the scanner with biofeedback, one of the novices already produced brain activation that was very similar to what we observed in our long-term practitioners. Another novice struggled on the first day of the in-scanner training to modulate the activity while producing feelings of loving-kindness; but on the second day, after receiving extensive biofeedback training, she was already able to activate the mental circuitry associated with states of loving-kindness in a much more controlled manner. Later studies showed that even without biofeedback in the scanner, after just one week of loving-kindness training, naive people could show an increase in networks previously identified only in the expert meditators.

We were also rather astonished to see the vast differences between people in their relative ability to cultivate compassion and loving-kindness. Some people are very good, and some have much more difficulty. It would be very interesting for us to know why.

Thupten Jinpa: I am quite puzzled by your experimental design, which involves modulating the intensity of compassion. This compassion is a result of training, but once you have arrived at that point, it's a spontaneous sort of feeling, and uncontrived. So you cannot talk about degrees.

Matthieu Ricard: Of course it's not natural, but the very purpose of the experiment was to see if you could modulate the intensity with which you concentrate on the suffering of others and generate compassion. When one vividly imagines someone suffering, compassion will arise. A process will take place during which compassion is born, then increases, and then finally reaches its full dimension. If you become distracted during that process, compassion might decrease and then later come back again. So there are gradations and variations. To voluntarily make your compassion grow or decline is artificial, of course, and in real life you would not want your compassion to decrease, but here we were doing it so that the researcher could measure it.

Tania Singer: In this early study, we wanted to know on the one hand what the neural circuitry of loving-kindness and compassion looks like. On the other hand, we also wanted to study people's ability to learn to regulate social emotions. For psychological research, understanding how people can learn to regulate their emotions is very important. The muscle in the brain that regulates emotion is always the same, no matter what the emotion is. So whether you train someone to up-regulate compassion or down-regulate anger or fear, using that muscle will enable that person to better regulate all of her emotions.

Let me now introduce another stream of research that is also concerned with emotional and motivational systems and how we can regulate them to achieve emotional balance and health. This research looks not only at brain responses but also at how hormones and neuropeptides can influence social emotions and social behavior like trust. Recent work has shown that if people are given certain hormones or neuropeptides, such as those that decrease one's sense of fear or increase the feeling of trust, people's social behavior may change. Finally, I want to show how this stream of research may link to the compassion research I have just spoken about.

Roughly speaking, we can distinguish between three basic types of motivational systems in the human brain. One we will call a *wanting* or *seeking system*, or an incentive-focused system. This system is associated with wanting, pursuing, achieving, consuming, with drive, excitement, and impatience. Many of the emotions connected with this system are positive—feelings of euphoria and wanting more.

Another system that's also very important for survival is what we call a *fear system*, or a threat-focused system. This is a system that acts very quickly in our brain when we perceive danger. For example, I am afraid of spiders, so when I see a spider, this system acts and I scream. This system is implicated in emotions of anger, anxiety, disgust, or panic. It can trigger a stress response in the body, which is associated with an increase in cortisol levels. Because of this, if you have chronic fear you can become ill, but normally this system is adaptive and primes us for feelings of self-protection and to seek safety when we are in danger.

The third system—and in our Western society we tend to forget a bit about this one—is the *caring system*, or the affiliation-focused system. Every animal has it. It's important for mother-child bonding, for connectedness, love, and contentment. Both the incentive-focused and the affiliative systems are associated with positive feelings, but the former is associated with high arousal and the latter with relaxation. What activates the caring system? In primates, grooming has been found to trigger this system. It is also associated with the release of a hormone and neuropeptide called *oxytocin*. Studies show that massage also activates oxytocin, which is why when you get a massage, you feel calm and soothed.

Interestingly, pro-social behavior can be motivated by the activation of any of these three systems. You can be pro-socially motivated by status, by fear, or by caring. I want to give you one example of how we have studied the interaction of the caring system with the fear system as a way to briefly show how these systems affect each other.

The part of the brain known as the *amygdala* is a crucial part of our fear and alarm system. High activation of the amygdala can lead to stress in the body, but oxytocin can down-regulate the activity of the amygdala. Oxytocin is very important in animals for mother-child bonding and for caring and attachment. If you remove receptors for oxytocin from the brains of prairie wolves, they will no longer create caring relationships with other wolves. Oxtyocin is a neurotransmitter crucial to mediating social bonding and attachment. If we give oxytocin to humans through a nasal spray, we can see in brain-imaging studies that it also reduces fear-related activation of the amygdala. For example, if I were to see a spider after receiving oxytocin, I would feel much better than I normally would when I see something I'm afraid of. We've done some related experiments with trust games. Ernst will talk about them later in detail,[4] but basically what we have found is that if you give oxytocin to people before they have to make a decision related to trust—in this case, whether to trust that a stranger will reciprocate an act of economic sharing—their trusting behavior increases significantly.

Dalai Lama: This shows that the different emotions completely depend on biochemical processes in the brain. In Buddhism, one of the purposes of practice is to try to reduce that dependency. As mental power increases, the mind is not entirely dependent on physical elements or biochemical processes. I think it's really worthwhile to test this oxytocin on Matthieu. But first you should give him one guarantee: that it will not damage his practice. That's important; otherwise he's truly a guinea pig! (*laughter*)

Tania Singer: That is a key question, whether you can also induce the same process through mental practice alone.

Dalai Lama: Is something going on that is similar to what happens in hypnosis? Hypnosis does not involve any use of hormones. . . .

Tania Singer: That's a good question; I don't know. We do know that you can decrease pain sensation through hypnosis. Hypnosis can reduce pain by activating the opiate system, which is also associated to the quiescence and caring system.

My question for you, Your Holiness—and we will also try answering this in our laboratory—is whether the induction and cultivation of compassion is a more efficient tool than the intake of oxytocin, because of course we don't carry oxytocin bottles in our pockets in normal life. If compassion activates this system, does it both reduce the subjective sensation of pain and reduce fear and anxiety? Is that plausible?

Dalai Lama: Definitely, yes. My understanding is that the way Buddhist training seems to act upon these processes is not by reducing the intensity of the actual feeling and emotions, but rather by expanding the field of our awareness so that there is a greater understanding of the framework. When we can see a bigger goal, we feel a tendency, a willingness, to sacrifice a smaller goal. So in meditation, the feeling of pain is reduced. From the Buddhist point of view, we would not see this as actually losing the intensity of the pain, but rather that the mind is not so focused upon the pain and sensation because it is paying full attention to the object of meditation instead. That's why you see that when someone who is worried or in physical pain goes on a picnic or listens to beautiful music, during that time his feeling of pain is reduced. It's a kind of redirecting.

Tania Singer: This is very interesting. We will perform these experiments in the future and hope to tell you about the results in some later conference.

3

The Neural Bases of Compassion

Richard Davidson

Richard Davidson is a professor of psychology and psychiatry, director of the Waisman Laboratory for Brain Imaging and Behavior, and founder and chair of the Center for Investigating Healthy Minds at the University of Wisconsin—Madison. A member of the Mind and Life Institute's board of directors since 1991, he has pioneered the scientific study of how contemplative practice affects the brain.

Richie presented data on the neurological basis of differences in empathy, altruism, and pro-social behavior among children, expert practitioners in compassion meditation, and in individuals who have undergone compassion training. His research shows a clear correlation between levels of activation in the insula and the amygdala and predisposition to pro-social behavior.

Your Holiness, it's wonderful to be with you again today. I would like to share with you a little bit about the work we've been doing with empathy and compassion in a variety of settings, beginning to look at the relationship between what we see in the brain and decisions that people make on certain economic tasks.

Let me begin with just two big points; the whole talk will really be about these two points. One is that people differ in what psychologists call *trait levels* of empathy and compassion. By "trait" here we mean consistent differences among people that persist over time. These differences are associated with underlying differences in biological characteristics. The second point is that according to modern neuroscience, empathy and compassion can be regarded as the product of skills that can be enhanced through training, and this training induces what we call *plastic changes* in the brain as well as in the body.

I want to distinguish between three kinds of empathy. The first is *negative valence empathy*, which is the tendency to experience feelings of concern or pain in response to another person's suffering. *Positive valence empathy* is the tendency to express positive emotion in response to another person's suffering, as a means to alleviate the other person's suffering, and to instill a positive emotional state in the other. The third variety is one we don't usually talk about in the scientific literature on empathy; it would be considered one of the four *brahmavihāras*[1] in Buddhism. This is *sympathetic joy*, which is the tendency to experience feelings of goodwill and pleasure in response to another person's feelings of happiness.

I want to discuss some work that we have not previously described to Your Holiness on studies conducted with young children. One of the wonderful things about studying young children is that they are not socialized like adults, so they are much more expressive, typically, than adults. You can actually see things in their behavior that are more difficult to see in adults, so you can clearly identify how they are reacting.

In our experiments with children, first we have them do a little imitation of how they comb their hair. Then the experimenter feigns hurting him- or herself on a clipboard. The experimenter exclaims about how he's injured his finger, it's turning red, and it really hurts, and then a few seconds later says it's starting to feel better. And we observe the reaction of the children. We've tested more than three hundred children between the ages of four and five years old. Some children react with a classic concerned face and elements of a fear grimace but show no display of positive emotion. So the experimenter is showing pain, and the child is just showing feelings of concern and negative emotion, which we consider to be negative valence empathy.

Another child hears the experimenter is feeling better and says, "That's good" or "That's awesome" with an enthusiastic smile. That's an example of positive valence empathy.

I share this to raise a question about the constituents early in life that may be the seeds of compassion. Two elements are evident. One is the experience of concern, and the second is a wish to cultivate the alleviation of suffering, to cultivate more positive emotion in the other who is suffering. Some children spontaneously show this. When you test three hundred children, you see lots of different patterns of behavior, and these patterns, these differences among the children, are associated with different measures of brain function that are directly predictive of their pattern of empathic response.

Now I want to move on to the circuits in the brain that are recruited when expert practitioners cultivate compassion. This is what Matthieu, who was one of the participating practitioners, said about this experiment: "What we have tried to do, for the sake of the experiment, is to generate a state in which love and compassion permeate the whole mind, with no other consideration, reasoning, or discursive thoughts. This is sometimes called *pure compassion*, *non-referential compassion* (in the sense that it does not focus on particular objects to arouse love or compassion), or *all-pervading compassion*."

The area in the brain that is circled here is the insula, the interoceptive cortex. This is one of the key areas of the brain that is modulated when expert practitioners cultivate compassion meditation in the laboratory. What we do to assess their brain state is present sounds that depict emotional episodes. Some of the sounds are negative sounds like a woman screaming or a baby crying. These are sounds of human suffering, and what we see is that among the expert practitioners, activity in this area of the brain is strongly increased when these sounds of suffering are presented. Novice practitioners who have just learned this practice show a little bit of increase, but only when they rate their meditation as being particularly good, or when they are relatively undistracted and focused on the awareness of compassion.

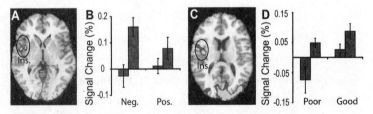

Figure 3.1: The brain image illustrates the greater activation of the insula, a region important for interoception, in long-term practitioners of compassion meditation when they generate compassion in response to distressing sounds such as a woman screaming or a baby crying.

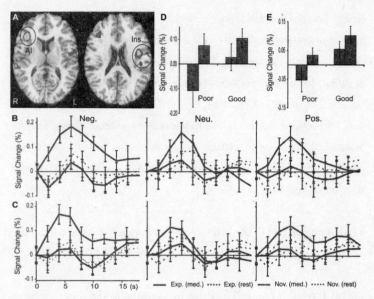

Figure 3.2: Fifteen expert meditators and fifteen age-matched controls participated in the experiment. The bottom row of figures depicts the signals in the insula for the experts (mainly higher lines) and the novices (mainly lower lines) in response to negative (left), neutral (middle), and positive (right) sounds. Solid lines depict the signal during compassion meditation periods and dotted lines depict the signals during a rest period. Note that only for the experts during compassion meditation is the signal in the insula higher than during rest, especially in response to negative sounds.

The amygdala is also part of the affected network. The amygdala has been implicated in many different aspects of emotional processing, but often with negative emotions; and yet the amygdala is strongly activated in expert practitioners during the practice of compassion in response to the sounds of suffering. It may be—and this is one of the questions that I'd love to explore with you, Your Holiness—that the cultivation of equanimity in the advanced practitioners allows them to respond to the negative emotional sounds strongly (as reflected in a large amygdala response), but also to recover more quickly. Indeed, in some recent studies with long-term meditation practitioners, we have found that their amygdala response to negative stimuli recovers more quickly than that of novices. In fact, the number of hours of lifetime practice among the expert practitioners corresponds to the extent to which we see these changes in the brain. In the novice practitioners, we don't see this. In the novice practitioners, the amygdala response is actually decreased rather than increased.

Thupten Jinpa: In the case of long-term practitioners, part of the process involves reducing attachment, so that could explain it.

Dalai Lama: It is quite clear that in compassion and concern, there is a biased sense and an unbiased sense. The biased one very much deals with "me," this is something nice to "me." The unbiased one is very objective.

Thupten Jinpa: Because the practice of cultivating equanimity involves that initial stage of detachment from the kind of attachment that we feel.

Dalai Lama: It reduces the partiality.

Richie Davidson: Your Holiness, I'd like to now move on to some new findings in novice practitioners, where we train them over the course of just two weeks. These are individuals who have never practiced before. They sign up for a research study where they are told they are going to be given an intervention that is designed to improve their well-being. They are randomly assigned either to a group that gets training in compassion and loving-kindness or to a group that gets training based on cognitive therapy, which involves teaching people to reappraise a negative situation and imagine that there is a positive outcome to the negative situation.

One of the questions we've explored is whether compassion varies according to the target object, and so after the training we have participants practice compassion for a loved one, for themselves, for a stranger, and for a difficult person. After two weeks of compassion training, the amount of compassion people report for a stranger and for a difficult person is comparable to what they reported for

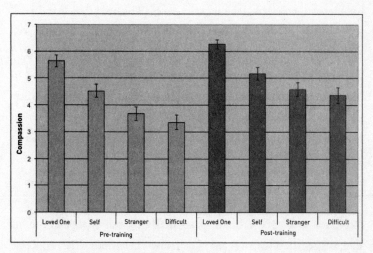

Figure 3.3: Participants were asked to rate the intensity of compassion they experienced on a 0–7-point scale where 0 reflects no compassion at all and 7 reflects the most intense levels of compassion they have ever experienced.

themselves before the training. The training, even though it's just thirty minutes a day for two weeks, induces this discernible change.

We also give them the task of an economic game; I'll describe it briefly in the interest of time. The key element here is that a person observes an economic interaction between two other participants. The interaction might be fair, or it might be unfair. If it's unfair, the participant has the opportunity to use some money that we have given him to redistribute the wealth to give the interaction a more altruistic outcome. That's the basic idea of the task.

What we find is that when we conduct this game with a large group of participants, people who redistribute more wealth report more empathic concern. They report greater feelings of warmth and compassion and concern for the suffering of others on the follow-up questionnaire. For example, they agree with the statement "I often have tender, concerned feelings for people less fortunate than I am." So this task has some validity in measuring empathic concern. We do brain scans on people before and after the two weeks of training. Then we give them the economic task at the end. What we find in the game is that the compassion group actually changes significantly more than the cognitive reappraisal group. They behave more altruistically on this economic decision-making task after just two weeks of training.

There's also a change in the brain after two weeks of training. Among the people in the compassion group, the amount of change in certain areas of the brain, particularly the amygdala and the insula, is associated with a change in altruistic behavior on the economic task. Compassion training down-regulates the amygdala; less amygdala signal at the second brain scan predicts greater distribution of

Redistribution Game

A. Step 1 : The Dictator can share their money with the recipient

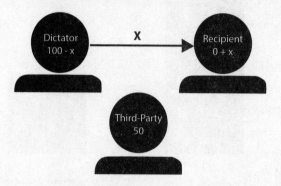

B. Step 2 : The Third-Party can pay to redistribute money from the Dictator to the Recipient.

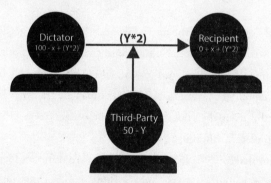

Figure 3.4: In the redistribution game, one participant, the dictator, is given $100. She can give money to the second participant, the recipient; and whatever she doesn't give, she gets to keep for herself. A third party is watching this interaction. The third party is given $50. She can use any or all of the money to more evenly distribute the dictator's original $100 between the dictator and the recipient. Whatever she gives will be doubled, taken from the dictator, and given to the recipient. She can also choose to keep the $50 for herself.

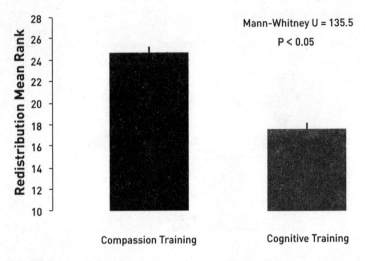

Figure 3.5.

wealth. When you put both the amygdala and the insula together, there's a very strong prediction. So the more change there is in the brain after two weeks of training, the more altruistically people behave, but only among the group that is given compassion training. The cognitive therapy group does not show any of these associations; their results are completely different.

Let me summarize. We've shown that there are different forms of compassion in young children, and we think some of these may represent the early seeds of empathic concern and altruistic behavior. Among experts, compassion meditation dramatically affects the brain's reactivity to stimuli that depict suffering, and among novices, two weeks of training changes the brain and increases altruistic behavior. Those people who show a greater change in the brain also show a greater change in altruistic behavior. And the patterns differ in experts and novices. The experts are able to remain with suffering and show high levels of amygdala activation, while novices reduce their amygdala activation with training. The former may be due to increased capacity for equanimity, or to the lack of attachment that Your Holiness described.

Collectively these findings illustrate how biology and experience shape our altruistic behavior in significant ways. But our levels of altruism and compassion are not fixed; the neural circuits associated with compassion are plastic. Through proper training, particularly training that begins early in life, we believe that we can promote compassion in a large segment of the population.

4

A Buddhist Perspective on Altruism

Matthieu Ricard

Matthieu Ricard is a Buddhist monk at Shechen Monastery in Kathmandu, Nepal. He holds a PhD in cellular genetics from the Pasteur Institute. He studied with eminent Tibetan teachers Kangyur Rinpoche and Dilgo Khyentse Rinpoche, and has served as French interpreter for His Holiness the Dalai Lama since 1989. A prolific writer and photographer, he devotes the proceeds from his books and much of his time to humanitarian projects in Tibet, Nepal, and India.

Matthieu's presentation illuminated Buddhist understandings of compassion, ignorance, suffering, and happiness. He described the emotional burnout of nurses who are constantly exposed to other people's suffering. Based on his own experience as a meditator and as a participant in Tania's research, he attested to compassion meditation and altruistic love as a potential antidote.

It is quite inappropriate to speak on a Buddhist subject in front of one's most respected teacher; but since such situations happen in modern life, I'll do it, even though it is like lighting a match in the bright sun. I ask forgiveness for that.

I would like to begin by offering a few definitions from the Buddhist perspective. *Altruistic love* is defined in Buddhism as the wish that all sentient beings might find happiness and the causes of happiness. When this unconditional benevolence is confronted with suffering, it naturally becomes *compassion*, which is the wish that all sentient beings be free from suffering and the causes of suffering. Altruistic love and compassion are not mere rewards for good behavior, and their absence is not punishment for bad behavior. Compassion means the desire to remove all forms of suffering, no matter what they are or who is experiencing them. So altruistic love and compassion are not contingent on the way people behave or the way they treat others. We can understand, from that perspective, how compassion could be extended to people who are not just your enemies, but even enemies of humanity—they are creating immense suffering for others, so a compassionate being wants to eradicate that suffering by all possible means.

What does it mean to have altruistic love or compassion for a tyrant? It doesn't mean that we like this person, approve of his behavior, or wish him success, saying, "After all, he's not such a bad guy; let's send him for a holiday in the Bahamas." To have compassion for a tyrant is to wish to remove the very causes that made him such an unpleasant person, thinking, "May the hatred, may the greed, may the cruelty, may the indifference be wiped out from this person's mind." That's the best wish we can make for humanity. And that's the best wish we can make for that person as well. So in this system, compassion and altruism are not moral judgments but are entirely directed toward removing suffering and fostering happiness. Of course moral judgments can, and should, be made, but they should not interfere with compassion or diminish it.

That is why altruism doesn't have to be biased. It doesn't have to be restricted to those we hold dear, or to those who treat us or others well. It applies to all sentient beings without exception. It does require deeply valuing the welfare of others, of all sentient beings. Again, it's not just our dear ones, not even just human beings. The way we treat animals, for instance, often reveals our incapacity to imagine the suffering of others. When you take a fish out of water, you don't imagine it is the same as if you were caught in the water with an iron hook. You are unable to put yourself in the situation of a fish and imagine how it would feel to endure what the fish endures. Taking the other's perspective is the foundation of valuing the sameness of all sentient beings. I don't want to suffer. Nobody wakes up in the morning thinking, "May I suffer the whole day, and if possible, my whole life." The most fundamental right of all sentient beings is to not suffer. We first recognize this in ourselves and then recognize it for others, which brings about a feeling of concern for all beings. That is essential.

Beyond that, when we say that compassion is about removing suffering and its causes, we also have to understand what the causes of suffering are. Suffering in Buddhist terms does not simply refer to a painful headache or even to a terrible massacre. According to Buddhism, much deeper causes of suffering are found in the distortion of reality, in not seeing things the way they are. Such distortion inevitably occurs when we superimpose our hatred, craving, and mental delusions onto reality. So the root cause of suffering here is what we call *ignorance*. Such ignorance is not just a lack of information, like not knowing the whole telephone directory by heart. It's a much deeper ignorance about the nature of reality, about not recognizing the impermanence of all phenomena, about perceiving the self as an autonomous, unitary, lasting entity, and all such distortions that eventually lead to suffering.

Can altruism be taught? Can compassion be taught? Yes, they can, because the mind has a potential for transformation that we vastly underestimate. We know that we aren't born knowing how to read and write and play the piano and all kinds of things, and we accept spending fifteen years or more on our education. Yet somehow we imagine that human qualities like compassion and altruism are innate. "That's just the way I am," people say. But contemplative experience as well as modern neuroscience show that we can change. Of course change will not happen simply because we wish for it—we must do something about it. Altruistic love and compassion need to be cultivated like any other skill.

There's no point in explaining too much of this view in front of His Holiness, so I just want to link these ideas with the science and the research to help advance a dialogue between these fields. We often hear people speaking about the compassion fatigue that affects caregivers such as nurses or people who care for those in need. Such people can become emotionally exhausted after being constantly and repeatedly exposed to the suffering of others. Tania's and other people's research has shown that when we perceive the suffering of others, the areas of our brain that are activated are similar to those that are activated in the person who suffers in front of us. It's not just our imagination; we really suffer.

So imagine the situation of a nurse. His or her suffering patients will hopefully be cured, or they might die; fortunately, it's rare that patients keep on enduring terrible suffering for years on end. But a caregiver who is exposed to the suffering of others day after day, patient after patient, will suffer every day along with every patient. He or she is actually suffering all the time through empathic resonance, and that sometimes leads to burnout, or the complete emotional exhaustion of compassion fatigue.

So what do caregivers do? Either they leave the job—"It's too much"—or they decide, "I cannot be so emotional." They create an emotional distance between themselves and their patients, which is not good. So is there any other way? We explored that question in our research with Tania. The task she gave us was to focus on visualizing and feeling the suffering of others without letting altruistic love and compassion grow. Of course, as His Holiness said, in a normal situation compassion will arise in a completely spontaneous and natural manner, but for the purposes of the experiment we tried to focus again and again just on the fact of the suffering. So what was the result? Within an hour or two, I personally felt a complete sense of burnout, distress, and powerlessness. The more you feel the suffering of others through empathy, without the dimension of altruistic love, the more your courage drains away and you break down. This was quite a surprise for me, but it also led to a great personal insight on the crucial difference that love and compassion can make.

After some time, Tania would direct me to shift from mere attention to suffering to compassion meditation. It felt like breaking a dam that released a flood of altruistic love. The image I had in my mind was that every atom of the suffering of others was being replaced by an atom of loving-kindness and compassion. That brought a complete change of experience. The suffering is still there, and you feel it, but now it's completely embraced by this much vaster perspective of positive, constructive, courageous altruistic love.

So it seems that what we called *stand-alone empathy* in that experiment, just resonating with suffering, can lead to unbearable distress. It is a little bit like an electric pump that keeps running without water flowing inside: it quickly gets hot and burns. There are some nurses who are naturally extremely loving and compassionate, so they don't burn out. But for other people, the kind of training that Richie and Tania discussed—which shows that one can bring about significantly more empathic concern and a more genuine sense of care within just a few weeks—could make a huge difference. This kind of loving-kindness and compassion training could bring immense good to the medical world and help caregivers to fulfill their vocation in ways that would be much more beneficial for their patients and themselves.

5

Biological Imperatives for Survival
Altruism Reconsidered

Joan Silk

Joan Silk is a professor at the School of Human Evolution and Social Change at Arizona State University and former chair of the Department of Anthropology at the University of California, Los Angeles. She is interested in how natural selection shapes the evolution of social behavior in non-human primates, and the evolutionary roots of capacities that play a crucial role in human societies, such as reconciliation, cooperation, friendship, paternal investment, and pro-social sentiments.

Various animals, including apes and bees, display altruistic and pro-social patterns of behavior; but do these patterns indicate motivation and choice, or are they simply biological imperatives for survival? After Joan reviewed research on choice and altruism in apes, the group discussion turned to comparisons of humans and animals, particularly the ability to feel gratitude and to grasp the long-term implications of one's actions.

I want to present some data that zoologists have collected about the way altruism is expressed in animals, and compare that with what we see in humans. As we have seen, many of the disciplines represented here have different definitions of altruism, so I'd like to begin by explaining what biologists mean when they use the word *altruism*.

Our current understanding of what motivates other animals to behave altruistically is still quite incomplete, but some of the preliminary answers suggest that there may be important differences between humans and other animals. The biological definition of altruism is influenced by our understanding of evolutionary theory. When biologists talk about altruism, we're thinking about behaviors that are beneficial to the recipient and costly to the actor, and that's similar to what we mean when we use the term generally. But in this case, instead of talking about money, we are talking about a currency that we call *genetic fitness*, which is an individual's ability to survive and to reproduce.

Altruism turns out to be reasonably common in other animals. We can see examples of altruism in many different animals in the animal kingdom. I study primates, and the most common form of altruism in primates is grooming.

Why exactly are they doing this? What's going on inside their heads? We don't know what the motives of the animals are, but we do know a lot of other things about the pattern of this behavior. We know how common it is, and we know something about who does it to whom. We also know that this kind of behavior is really good for the animals. If we measure how social individuals are, the long-term data shows that females who are the most sociable have the highest fitness. Their infants are most likely to survive.

This evidence tells us that being social is good for females in some ways, but altruism in primates is still more limited than it is in humans.

Figure 5.1: An adult male chimpanzee grooms another male. Grooming is the most common form of cooperative behavior in primates. Other forms of cooperation include food sharing, alliance formation, and territory defense.

It tends to be directed toward relatives and reciprocating partners. It's limited to group members, and the number of individual primates who can cooperate together is quite small compared to humans.

We know a lot about the patterns of altruism in humans, and now we've begun to ask what motivates this kind of altruism in other animals. It could be compassion. It could be a sense of justice. It could be because they care about fairness, or because they have concern for others. Or it could be something else. They could lack all these things and still perform altruistic behaviors. To find out about motives, we need to go beyond our own interpretations of what the animals are doing.

In 1996, a child fell into the gorilla cage at a zoo in Chicago.[1] A female gorilla picked the child up in her arms and carried him to the back of the enclosure. Why did she do that? Maybe she did it because she saw that the child was in danger and she wanted to help; that's the interpretation people usually give. But one thing that I found out from talking to the people at the zoo is that when she was very young, this gorilla was trained by zookeepers on how to take care of a baby. (In zoos, gorilla mothers sometimes don't know how to care for their young.) They trained her to carry her child like this, and they trained her to bring it to them so they could see if the baby was okay.

So how do we find out what the gorilla was thinking when she did this? What we've begun to do is to try to investigate the question in a more systematic way by conducting experiments to determine whether or not helpfulness is based on concern for the welfare of others. To do this, we've borrowed some logic from economic experiments. We give an individual two choices, and the choices have different rewards. The choices tell us something about the animal's preferences. If somebody offers me carrots or celery and I choose celery, then you think I prefer celery to carrots. This is exactly what we do with the apes.

This is one experiment we conducted with a pair of chimpanzees. Their roles in the context of the experiment are actor and partner. The actor has two choices. One choice brings one banana for the actor and one banana for his partner. The other choice brings one banana for the actor and nothing for the partner. Somewhat surprisingly, the chimps choose at random, equally, between these two choices.

We have reason to think that chimps understand how this works, which is of course a very important thing, because otherwise the experiment is not very useful. We have done this experiment repeatedly, and we've now done it with many chimpanzees from many different groups, not just one very unkind chimpanzee.

This kind of experiment gives us some idea about preferences. It looks like even though chimpanzees can be very altruistic in their day-to-day behavior, they may not have the same kinds of motives for

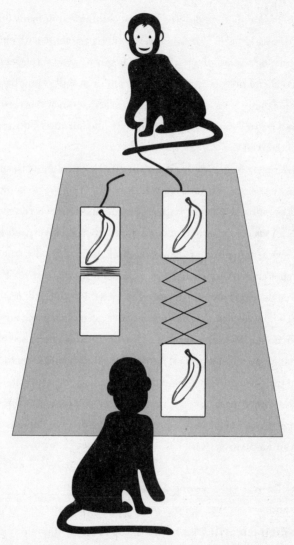

Figure 5.2: The chimps have two options: (1) they can take one banana for themselves and one banana for the other chimp or (2) they can take one banana for themselves and no banana for the other. Research shows that chimpanzees do not prefer the generous option (1).

their behavior that we do. To see how chimps and humans may differ in this way, we've also done a series of experiments with children. By about four years of age, children begin to show preferences for the pro-social option. Sometimes the children will even give up rewards for themselves to give rewards to others, even at this very young age; and there's some evidence that they like fair distributions more than unfair ones.

We're just beginning to explore motives in other animals, and even with primates our answer is not yet complete. What we do know about primates is that we begin with a primate ancestor who's very, very social; forms very strong bonds, particularly to relatives; and is quite cooperative, but restricts the scope of altruism. We also know that these apes are smarter than monkeys, and more cooperative. The apes can even develop relationships based on trade. But they still don't show as much concern for the welfare of others as children and adults do.

In humans we see a number of features that we don't see in other apes: language, culture, moral norms, compassion, and so forth. We're still in the process of understanding how similar or how different we are from other primates, but there is some evidence that this capacity for compassion is much more highly developed in humans than in even our closest relatives.

Dalai Lama: Encouraging. Hopeful signs.

Matthieu Ricard: Your Holiness, you often mention that extended altruism is based on biological altruism. What I mean by "biological" or "natural" altruism is the one we inherited through evolution, which is best exemplified by parental and especially motherly love. As you have often said, this is a wonderful love that is natural and does not need to be trained. But it remains biased, because it applies to our offspring first, and then extends, to some degree, to our other relatives, and then perhaps to those who treat us well.

It is very difficult for such altruistic love to extend to strangers and even more so to difficult people who harm us or harm others. But you have explained on many occasions that cognitive training based on reasoning and wisdom can make one understand that all beings without exception wish to be free from suffering, and that we should be concerned about all of them. This allows the arising of a much more extended form of altruistic love. This kind of altruism requires training, but it is unbiased, and it is based on recognizing the deeper causes of suffering that we mentioned earlier. Can you say a few words about how to move from limited, biased altruism to extended altruism?

Dalai Lama: First, compassion is related to intelligence. So maybe we can say it this way: less intelligent mammals and even birds cannot see holistically. This means seeing not only the present, but also possible future consequences. With intelligence, you can see more holistically.

A flower, a plant, is very beautiful, but it has no feeling or cognition, so it has no way to cultivate compassion. Only sentient beings experience pain and pleasure; that's the basis of compassion. And with the help of intelligence, compassion can be enhanced. Whether God created us or nature created us, we are social animals. Have you ever tested bees as a social animal?

Joan Silk: Well, we know they're incredibly social and can only survive in the social world.

Dalai Lama: Has any experimental work been done observing the behavior of bees within their own colony versus with bees from outside the colony?

Joan Silk: In many animals, there is extended altruism within the colony, but if an outsider comes in they're very hostile.

Dalai Lama: If a few bees from this colony and that colony are put in the same area for a longer period, can they eventually mix, or not?

Joan Silk: No, they can't.

Dalai Lama: I'm wondering whether that hostility and that kind of discrimination is simply a function of lacking familiarity, of not having been connected. Can they come into contact and become familiar with time? Of course, the colony's survival does not depend on outsiders, so they consider outsiders hostile. But is there any circumstance in which if two groups are put together, they eventually make hives, build a new colony, develop a new group? Is there the possibility of change in these tiny insects' minds, in different circumstances?

Joan Silk: I'm not hopeful.

Dalai Lama: You're not? There's something very fixed biologically that cannot change?

Joan Silk: I think that it's fixed biologically in an animal like a bee. They don't have much flexibility in their behavior. What distinguishes us so clearly from animals with such small brains is flexibility. They're programmed genetically, and there's not much flexibility in their behavioral repertoire.

Dalai Lama: Don't some mammals have some form of language, some way to signal each other? How much does their brain function differ from that of animals that have no language?

Joan Silk: You mean the difference in flexibility of behavior?

Dalai Lama: Yes.

Joan Silk: Those animals have very large brains, very flexible behavior, and great capacity for social learning and potentially for very elaborate social behavior. There are some animals that you would like to test and ask if they're pro-social, because it may be something about the kind of world they live in and the kinds of groups they live in that would promote that kind of behavior. I don't think it's a limit on how smart apes are. I think it's a limit based on the kind of world they've evolved in.

Dalai Lama: For my own curiosity, if you give me permission to ask this question: What is the relationship between appreciation and altruism? Do you see a link between the appreciation of another's kindness and altruistic behavior?

Joan Silk: I think that altruism, doing something that's good for someone else, doesn't require a lot of understanding or appreciation of others.

Matthieu Ricard: What His Holiness asks is whether the recipient of altruism appreciates what you do and feels some kind of gratitude.

Joan Silk: Oh! It's a wonderful question. They appreciate receiving the behavior. The female being groomed obviously appreciates the feeling of being groomed, but whether or not there's any sense of gratitude or appreciation toward the groomer, we don't know.

Dalai Lama: But you see, I still have not gotten the answer. Like the mosquito—it seems to show no sense of appreciation. Many animals, if we feed them, if we show them sincere love, they appreciate it. But mosquitoes—when my mood is good and I feel sure that there is no danger of getting malaria, I give some blood to the mosquito, but afterward there's no sign of appreciation! On many occasions I've asked professors and scientists about this. I wonder whether the pro-social behavior we see among bees can actually be characterized as altruistic behavior, because if it's fixed, then it's really purely biologically driven. I was wondering whether characterizing that behavior as altruistic is accurate. Non-sentient beings, plants, also have some capacity to adjust to their environment, to respond to crowding and so on. It's a purely chemical, biological process. So in a very, very tiny animal, maybe it's just biological, for survival? It's almost like automatic behavior.

Joan Silk: Sure, sure. But I think this is a question you're better able to answer than I am.

Dalai Lama: I'm also ignorant about this. I'm just guessing. I don't know. Perhaps I may add a little bit. I think a holistic view may be the main factor. With more intelligence, you can see a wider picture, which then allows for a concern for others' well-being, appreciation, and helping to arise. Sometimes we human beings, because of our intelligence and our ability to hold a long-sighted or holistic view, can make immediate sacrifices and be willing to take on hardships for some long-term benefit. Animals may in some cases be able to think in terms of their interest for the next year, or the next month, or for their offspring, but otherwise I don't think they have that capacity to see the future holistically. So with regard to compassion, I think that human beings' care for each other is biologically essential for our survival. For another person to bring energy and effort toward someone else's survival, there has to be a will on his or her part. That comes from altruism, affection, love, a sense of responsibility. Of course, that is closely related to attachment, but that's okay.

PART II

Economic Research on Altruism and Pro-Social Behavior

6

The Social Dilemma Experiment

Ernst Fehr

Ernst Fehr is a professor of microeconomics and experimental economics and chairman of the Department of Economics at the University of Zurich. His research combines insights from economics, social psychology, sociology, biology, and neuroscience to shed light on sociological and psychological aspects of modern economics.

Fehr's social dilemma experiment, which tracks both people's trust in altruism and real altruism, disproves the long-standing supposition that only self-interest motivates economics. In his presentation he also introduced the idea of altruistic sanctioning, and demonstrated the value of accountability in social obligations.

Thank you very much for the opportunity to present my work to His Holiness. I want to first talk about what altruism is according to economists. My definition is the following: if a person acts in a way that is costly for herself but provides a benefit to someone else, the person's behavior is altruistic. The actor is not motivated by direct or indirect future material benefits associated with the act, but she may still experience a psychological benefit. She may feel better because she engaged in the altruistic act, but according to this definition, that does not prevent it from being altruistic.

Let me give you an example. If I incur economic costs in order to care for my children, my friends, or the victims of a catastrophe, I behave altruistically if I do it regardless of any potential future economic benefit, such as a tax rebate. Even if I have a good feeling when I give money to a charity, that's still an altruistic act.

Now, does altruism exist according to this definition? I want to cite two Nobel Prize winners in economics. One is George Stigler, who won the prize in 1982. He said, "When self-interest and ethical values with wide verbal allegiance are in conflict much of the time, most of the time, in fact, self-interest-theory will win."[1] Oliver Williamson, who won the prize in 2009, made an even stronger statement: "Humans are self interest-seeking with guile, which includes more blatant forms such as lying, stealing, and cheating, but more often involves subtle forms of deceit."[2]

Dalai Lama: This is really pessimistic!

Ernst Fehr: It's important to emphasize that these are mere beliefs. A whole profession got hooked on these beliefs! But they are not substantiated by facts. So when people wrote down these words, they did not know, they just *believed* them to be the case. And when I started my research twenty or twenty-five years ago, this was the prevailing attitude in economics. So for a long time, only a few economists thought to study altruism. At best it was considered a rarely occurring anomaly amid otherwise standard, self-interested behavior.

My colleagues and I have long disagreed with this view, and for

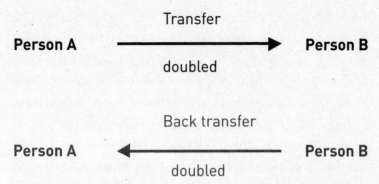

Figure 6.1: Two strangers are paired anonymously; each receives $10. Person A can give person B up to $10; the experimenter doubles the amount given. Person B then has the chance to give money back to person A. This voluntary, sequential exchange happens only once, and the strangers never meet face-to-face.

years we have been conducting research on altruism in economic interactions. As other presenters have suggested, it can be difficult to study altruism empirically. But I want to present to you a typical experiment that we have conducted that has had interesting results. I call it a *social dilemma experiment*. Sometimes it's also called a *trust game* or a *trust experiment*, and you will see why.

The experiment goes as follows. Two strangers are paired anonymously. Each one receives an endowment of $10. Person A can transfer between $0 and $10 to person B. The experimenter then doubles that amount. So if I send His Holiness $1 in this experiment, His Holiness will receive $2. If I send $10, he will receive $20. Now person B can transfer money back, also between $0 and $10, and this is again doubled by the experimenter. (See figure 6.1.)

This experiment looks artificial, but in fact what we are capturing here is an economic exchange. I have a good that you value more, and you have a good that I value more. If we exchange the goods, we are both better off. The trick is that this happens sequentially: I have to go first, and you can go second. In principle, if I send you all my money, you can say thank you and keep it, and send me back nothing. We never meet again. We are strangers to each other. You have no future gain from being nice to me. There is no way you could benefit materially by giving me your money, because you have already received my money. That's the reason we can evaluate your transfer to me as an altruistic act, because there is nothing but altruism that can cause you to make that transfer.

If person B gives something back, this is a nice measure of altruism, but we also learn something else from this transaction. If person A believes that person B is altruistic, person A has a reason to make a transfer, because the money doubles during the exchange. Thus person A's transfer measures his trust in other people's altruism. So we have two very important things that we measure here: trust in other people's altruism, and real altruism. Let's see what people do in this experiment.

Dalai Lama: If the first person gives $5, the other person now has $20, because he's got $10 plus $5, and then $5 is added by the experimenter.

Ernst Fehr: Yes.

Dalai Lama: Now he could just walk off with just the $20. He has nothing to lose here.

Ernst Fehr: Yes. It is very important that we understand that these are two strangers who never meet.

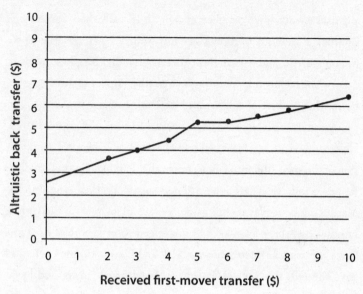

Figure 6.2.

We did this experiment with a representative population in Germany of roughly one thousand people. Let's see what they do.

If person A sends $2, then person B sends back, on average, $3.50. If person A sends $10, person B sends back, on average, $6.50. The important thing is that this is altruism, even though there's an inequality here.

One might now say, "Well, $10, what's $10? It's not very much. Maybe it's easy to be altruistic because it's only $10." But if we do this experiment with $100, the same thing happens. If we do these experiments with up to three months' income, people behave the same way. We couldn't do this experiment in Switzerland; that would have been too expensive. We had to go to a poor country where one hundred Swiss francs is a lot of money. Our data clearly show that altruism is not a low-cost phenomenon. It is really there, even when significant amounts of money are involved. We can observe it, we can measure it, and we can measure trust in other people's altruism.

I want to finish by pointing out another aspect of altruistic behavior that is more novel. We call it *altruistic sanctioning*, or *altruistic punishment*. It's an interesting term, because it sounds self-contradictory. How can I be altruistic when I punish somebody? There is an extension of the social dilemma experiment that will explain this concept. It goes as follows: There is a third person, an observer, who watches Matthieu and me playing this game. We are anonymous to each other, but the observer—let's say it's Tania—can observe both of us. Tania observes that Matthieu sends me $10, and I send nothing back. So I have cheated, in a sense. Matthieu trusted my altruism, and I sent back nothing. The interesting aspect of this extended experiment is that Tania has the option to punish me. How? She has some money, and she can spend $1 to destroy $3 of mine.

Why should she punish me? There's an implicit obligation between Matthieu and me: when Matthieu sends me money, I should send him something back. So Tania might want to punish me because I have violated a social obligation. And this is important, because if she punishes me today, I might not cheat someone else tomorrow, because I know there are others out there who may sanction my selfish behavior. That's the subtle way in which this sanction has an altruistic function, because it makes me behave more pro-socially in the future.

Richie [Davidson] described a related experiment in his presentation, but there are a few important differences. In his redistribution game, the transfer is one way—person A gives money to person B, but person B cannot give anything back—whereas here, there is the potential for reciprocity. The social dilemma experiment also adds a dimension of "trust" that is not present in the redistribution game. Finally, in the extended social dilemma experiment, the third party cannot redistribute money between the other two parties. Instead the third party can only sanction person B.

Dalai Lama: This is quite similar to the Buddhist understanding of the value of punishment, within the monastic discipline for example, so that the person does not get into the bad habit of doing something again in the future

Ernst Fehr: I completely agree. We also do this with our children sometimes; we punish out of an altruistic motivation, because we want to prevent bad habits from forming.

Dalai Lama: I often give an example from my own childhood: when I was a student, my tutor used to keep a whip next to him. That's harsh altruism!

Ernst Fehr: Now the question is, does Tania spend money in the experiment to make me more pro-social? What we find is that people do. In fact, roughly 50 percent of the people in this experiment behaved that way. They punished altruistically. And those findings have very important implications for economic and social life, which we will describe in more depth later. For now, what's important is that many people have trust in others' altruism, and in fact a substantial share of people behaves altruistically.

One of the key questions that has not been solved but may be solved in part by Tania and Richie and others is, to what extent can we change people's motivation and personality? Almost all of us have also observed that many people do behave selfishly. They do not behave altruistically. This is very important, because it forces us to think about how we can channel the behavior of selfish people to pro-social goals.

Let me say, finally, why this is important. Altruism provides social insurance; altruists help if help is needed. That's very important. In the absence of a welfare state, only altruism is left. In fact, you can argue that the welfare state itself is partly a result of altruistic efforts.

Altruism also increases the volume of mutually beneficial economic exchanges. Why? Because we are more willing to keep obligations if there are people in society who behave altruistically, or who punish altruistically. Altruism helps enforce the cooperative norms that are at the very basis of human culture, and of modern democracy and individual liberties.

7

First Thoughts Toward
a Buddhist Economics

John Dunne

John Dunne is an associate professor in the Department of Religion at Emory University, where he is cofounder of the Emory Collaborative for Contemplative Studies. His work focuses on various aspects of Buddhist philosophy, cognitive science, and contemplative practice, and he frequently serves as a translator for Tibetan scholars.

According to Tibetan Buddhism, true happiness is based on internal resources that, with the right knowledge, perspective, and practice, can be cultivated without limit. John explained how these resources can be promoted through secular training, and shared a model for a kind of Buddhist economics first proposed by Tara Tulku Rinpoche. John, His Holiness, and Ernst discussed whether it is more effective to transform individuals or systems and rules when promoting altruism.

As Matthieu said, it's always a rather difficult task to give a talk on Buddhism before His Holiness. If Matthieu was lighting a match in the sun, I'm afraid I'm lighting a wet match, but I will do my best.

We've been talking about the idea of cost and its relationship to altruism and compassion. For example, if Ernst and I were to play the extended trust game and Ernst were to give me $10, if I gave him back $5, from the definition that we've had so far, that would be considered an altruistic action. But why am I giving $5 back to Ernst? Because I am afraid that some other player in the game is going to punish me for being selfish. So my motivation there is not to benefit Ernst; my motivation is actually to protect myself.

From the Buddhist standpoint, it's very important for us to be able to distinguish between activities that are truly motivated by the aim to benefit the other and activities that may involve a cost but come from a different motivation. In Tibetan, the general term for motivation is *kun long*,[1] so what we're speaking about is *shen pen ge kun long*,[2] or "a motivation that seeks to benefit the other."

Part of what this means in terms of altruism, or altruistic actions, is that when we're seeking to benefit another, we could be doing so in the context of punishment. For example, if other players punish me in the extended trust experiment for not giving money back to Ernst, they might do so because they're angry with me. That would not be altruism from a Buddhist perspective. But if they punish me because they want to help me get rid of this bad habit, and they want me to benefit Ernst so I won't treat him like this again in the future, then it would be altruism. So the role of motivation, or *kun long*, is very central here.

Another question this raises is whether we can have purely altruistic action. This is not simply a matter of cost. If we put cost in the equation, pure altruism becomes difficult, but if we remove the issue of cost and look just at motivation, then pure altruism seems possible. Very briefly, the Buddhist view is that altruism always benefits an altruistic actor because it is a positive and healthy mental state. So an altruistic action with no benefit for the actor is actually impossible; it's a contradiction in terms. If we define altruism as an action that is solely intended to benefit the other, then pure altruism is possible, even if the altruistic person happens to get some unintended benefit too. To be clearer about all this, let's have a closer look at the cultivation of altruism and compassion in a Buddhist context.

A central goal of Buddhist practice is to cultivate the kind of motivational attitudes, dispositions, and habits that constitute compassion and altruism. When we talk about these practices, we're really in a Buddhist context, but there are also a number of different efforts and initiatives in place right now to develop secular styles of training for cultivating altruism and compassion. Thupten Jinpa is involved in such an effort at the Center for Compassion and Altruism Research and Education at Stanford University, and at Emory University, my colleague Geshe Lobsang Tenzin is involved in developing a secular training method for compassion. I know that Tania's and Richie's labs have been doing something similar. So there is great interest in asking what are the key ingredients that must be present in secular training in order for us to effectively cultivate compassion and the altruistic behaviors that come from compassion.

One of these key ingredients is the recognition of our fundamental equality or sameness. This idea is based on a sort of Buddhist axiom. One way of understanding human behavior is that there is a drive to reproduce. You might hear that in a biological context. But in a Buddhist context, what is driving sentient beings is actually a search for happiness. That axiom is what allows us to see everyone as equal to ourselves. In other words, the fact that we are all seeking happiness and seeking to avoid suffering makes us all equal, inasmuch as this is our common, fundamental motivation.

Seeing all beings as fundamentally equal in this way can eliminate the in-group/out-group distinction that makes our altruism and compassion partial and biased. What we need to be able to do, to use a sort of neuroscience lingo, is to take offline this in-group/out-group distinction and develop unbiased, universal compassion. We also need to look not just at short-term goals, but also at long-term goals. The capacity to do so is dependent on the use of our intelligence and on our use of conceptual tricks, or conceptual training. There is a wonderful summation of this in a text called the *chyun jug*[3] in Tibetan, or the *Bodhicaryāvatāra* [The Guide to the Bodhisattva's Way of Life], a seventh-century text by the great Buddhist Sanskrit poet and saint Śāntideva. In it he says, "Happiness is equally precious to others and myself, so what is so special about me that I strive after happiness for myself all alone?"[4] This type of conceptual training, actually a kind of cognitive reappraisal, is used very heavily as a precursor to the actual development of compassion in Buddhist practice.

Once we have a sense of equality among ourselves and others—in other words, when we have eliminated this in-group/out-group distinction—and when we have a broader and vaster sense of our long-term goal, then we can begin to expand our practice. His Holiness briefly mentioned one method of this earlier. In the Buddhist style of practice, one could visualize one's mother as a paradigm of someone truly loving, as someone who's going to activate what Tania refers to as the affiliative system, which is the neurobiological system that correlates with the natural sense of connection and empathy that one feels for one's in-group. In primates, this system appears to be especially strong in the connection between parent and offspring. Buddhist practices take advantage of this natural sense of connection and empathy by using a visualization of one's mother as a means to effectively activate that system. Then one uses a particular technique to extend those feelings to all sentient beings. There is a famous phrase that we find in Tibetan, *ma gyur sem chen tamché*,[5] which means "all sentient beings, my mothers." This is a very powerful means of taking the natural tendency toward compassion in the relationship between mother and child and extending it.

This practice depends very heavily on intelligence. It also depends a little bit on cultural factors. I've served as a translator on various occasions when this technique has been taught, and inevitably there will be some person in the U.S. who stands up and says, "But I don't really like my mother."

Dalai Lama: Even among Tibetans, we might find some people like that. Of course it depends on the mother also. Some mothers are really terrible mothers.

John Dunne: I'm happy to say my mother is a very good one.

Dalai Lama: Oh good! Mine too!

John Dunne: But whether it's one's mother or someone else, there is always someone who can bring these feelings online.

One thing we haven't spoken about is *why* we cultivate compassion from the Buddhist perspective. The claim here, and really it is an empirical claim, is that our innate self-centeredness distorts our cognition in ways that frustrate our search for happiness. In other words, our self-centeredness can distort our experience of the world in such a way that we don't understand the world clearly. And because we lack a clear understanding of the world, our attempts to become happy fail, precisely because they are based, in a sense, on very biased information.

By cultivating a concern for the other, by moving from self-centeredness to other-centeredness, one gives wisdom a chance; one gives oneself a greater chance to see the world clearly. And as a by-product of seeking to benefit others, one ends up cultivating happiness. There's a kind of paradox or irony here in that if one tries directly to cultivate one's own happiness—if I say, "I'm going to benefit Ernst so I can be happy"—it won't work. However, if my aim is truly to benefit Ernst, my own happiness will come along with that. This is the claim.

I'd like to quote another wonderful verse from Śāntideva: "All those who are unhappy in the world are so because they desire their own happiness. All those who are happy in the world are so because they desire others to be happy."[6] This is an amazing verse. It's also quite challenging, but it points to this notion that the happiest persons are those who are more focused on the happiness of others.

These are the two fundamental aspects of compassion practices in the Buddhist context. The first is the importance of intelligence, of gaining that broad perspective you have mentioned, Your Holiness, through eliminating the in-group/out-group distinction. The second is a visualization technique, recalling events or people to bring that affiliative system online, to give oneself a little dose of oxytocin, so to speak. The question is, are these two ingredients also key to effective secular training in compassion? Can they be used in a secular context?

Dalai Lama: Obviously, the whole world is now heavily interdependent. I think this is actually the new reality. The entire world is part of me; whether we like it or not, it has happened. Switzerland cannot remain isolated, entirely independent from the whole world, can it? You have a direct connection, at least to the European Union. That's the new reality, isn't it? Because of that new reality, an altruistic attitude must consider the whole rest of humanity as part of me; my future depends on them. I think the same goes for the need for universal secular ethics.

Here I'm not talking about my welfare in the next life or heaven, but just this life. I think earlier I mentioned that this is not just a Buddhist idea; according to believers of God, everything comes from one source. There's equality there. I think we can utilize this concept.

John Dunne: It's quite interesting to see that in the secular trainings that have been developed, these types of concepts are emerging naturally. They seem to be effective even without being in a religious context.

Dalai Lama: That's right.

John Dunne: They're effective in creating compassion and altruistic behaviors, but there is still another problem in the Buddhist context. Our fundamental problem is that we often misunderstand the nature of happiness and the true causes of happiness. We often end up chasing after external resources, instead of cultivating the internal resources that are necessary for happiness. This is not to say that external resources are not necessary, but by themselves they are not going to constitute the causes for happiness.

I'd like to talk briefly about a notion that I got from Tara Tulku Rinpoche some years ago about a kind of Buddhist economics. What we begin with is this premise: since what we seek is happiness, the most valuable resources are those that lead to this goal. The claim here—again, this is an empirical claim, one that can be investigated—is that those resources are primarily internal, and so these internal resources of happiness are of the highest value for us. That is fortunate, because those resources can be limitlessly cultivated by other-centered attitudes.

Economics can thus be shifted so that internal resources become central to our calculations. In other words, a sort of Buddhist economics would see these internal resources as relevant to our external economic exchanges, to our cost-benefit analyses. When we are looking at these types of cost-benefit calculations, we could say that a gain in external resources could come at an internal cost. This morning I had a discussion with Bill George, who said that at one time there was a notion that if one got angry in a business exchange, this could be an effective means of gaining more profit. The problem is that anger is actually going to come at a considerable internal cost. If one takes those internal resources into account, the cost-benefit analysis will change.

We can also speak of this in external terms. It is thought that emotions like anger can actually have an impact on one's health. So in a very direct way, if we fail to keep in mind the impact of our external actions on our internal resources, the results can be devastating.

Of course, a loss in external resources could constitute a considerable internal gain. The best example of this, in the Buddhist context, is generosity. If one gives a gift, there is a loss in external resources, but this act is thought to be cultivating precisely those types of other-centered internal resources that will lead to happiness. What that means is that generosity is always a win-win game. Externally the recipient wins, and internally the giver wins. I think this is perhaps the main message of this Buddhist economics—that there's a new way to configure our economic exchanges so that we have many more win-win opportunities.

Dalai Lama: If you use the phrase *Buddhist economics*, people may immediately get the impression we're talking about a kind of money-oriented economic system according to Buddhism, but if you called it *internal economics*, then there wouldn't be that confusion. But I am wondering whether that would actually be a legitimate use of the term *economics*. In the Buddhist concept, there is a notion of what are called the *seven noble riches, phak pai nor dün*,[7] but then these include trust, wisdom, ethical integrity, generosity, and so on. Can we actually use the term *economics* for these?

John Dunne: That's a very good question, Your Holiness. There are some scholars who have picked up this idea. I'll just point out a few references, because it was helpful for me to read their work and to speak with them. Maria Heim has written an excellent book on giving in the context of Buddhism;[8] and Andy Rotman points out that there really are many, many economic metaphors that are used to refer to these internal resources.[9] So I think perhaps we couldn't literally call them wealth, but maybe we can speak of them that way metaphorically.

The problem with calling this *internal economics* is that we're actually speaking about both the internal and the external. I don't mean to say that external exchanges are irrelevant—in fact they're very important for the practice of cultivating these internal resources in Buddhism.

Dalai Lama: Yes.

John Dunne: Giving, the act of generosity (*jin-pa thong-ba*[10]), is very important as a way of cultivating these internal resources, so maybe what we're speaking about is a kind of holistic economics that's both external and internal.

Dalai Lama: Holistic. That's very good.

Ernst Fehr: I have a question that's inspired by my thinking as an economist. As economists we are taught that you take people's preferences as given. You don't want to patronize them. What I mean by "preferences" are people's desires and goals. Now when economists think about improving society, making the world a better place, we think primarily about changing laws, changing institutions, changing regulations, and not about changing the individual.

For example, many people say that greed drove the economic crisis. That was certainly one factor behind the crisis. Of course that's part of the story, but how can I solve that problem? Should I send the greedy people to an educational camp and teach them to become altruists, or should I change the laws and regulations in such a way that their greedy desires are channeled in a pro-social way? As a social scientist, I typically go for the latter option. I want to change the laws, the social norms, the regulations. I want to provide a collective solution to the problem, not an individualized one.

My question to you is, how do you see this from a Buddhist perspective? What's the weight you put on changing people, versus the weight you put on changing society in the sense of changing its institutions and rules?

Dalai Lama: I think both, with equal emphasis. Unless people in general change, their way of life, their way of thinking—unless that takes place, no matter how beautiful your laws are, there will be corruption in some way. One of my Indian friends mentioned in a recent conversation that certain regulations at the federal level, as well as the state level, are very good, but the implementation is not. The people who are supposed to carry out these responsibilities are not properly carrying them out. Even though we might have beautiful resolutions on paper, if the actual people on the ground who are supposed to be implementing them don't behave in the way that they should, then it's very difficult.

And we can't blame these people alone; these people come from a society where there is not much emphasis placed on altruism or serious concern about others' well-being. People who come from that kind of society adopt those habits. So we need to work really at both levels, and at the grassroots level, in education. We often discuss the education system. If right from the beginning, from kindergarten, we create awareness in children, then eventually altruism becomes part of their habits. Then there is a real possibility to change society, eventually on a global level.

In some remote areas in India and in the past in Tibet also, there are communities where people never lock their doors, because the people are really self-disciplined and honest. There are no thieves! A hungry person can come take some food, and they will not complain. In some of these cases, maybe people are quite poor, so they have nothing to lose; but they are so open and trusting, any stranger can come and is welcome. They share equally. These are, of course, very small populations with very simple lifestyles. Sometimes a more luxurious, sophisticated life also increases greed. When on your side you increase greed, people on the other side also increase their greed, and then suspicion arises. These feelings automatically come.

Another Tibetan case: One of my friends is a very good monk, a very good practitioner, and he is now abbot of one of the monasteries in northern India. Once I visited his room and saw some sort of box that was not locked. I asked, "So you haven't locked these cupboards there?" He said, "I have nothing inside!"

This also reminds me a story about Milarepa, the famous Tibetan poet saint. He was in his cave one night when a thief came. Milarepa burst into laughter and said to the thief, "What can you find that I cannot find in daylight?"

8

The Economics of Happiness

Richard Layard

Lord Richard Layard is professor emeritus of economics at the London School of Economics. He was founder-director of its Centre for Economic Performance and now heads CEP's Wellbeing Programme. His work on unemployment, childhood, mental health, and well-being has influenced policy in Britain and beyond.

Many economic theorists have suggested that we need competition to drive economic growth, and that economic growth will also bring growth in happiness. In his session, Richard spoke about why happiness levels have flatlined, despite unprecedented increases in income and quality of life. William Harbaugh, His Holiness, and others joined in discussing how age, trust, life expectancy, and social comparison affect our happiness, and our potential to change our priorities on a societal and biological level.

Your Holiness, it's wonderful to be able to discuss these issues with you, especially at this time of economic reappraisal. What we are going to do in this session is look at the bigger picture, the whole economy, the whole of society. How should it be organized so as to produce conditions for the greatest happiness of the population? This is the basic question that economic theory has been trying to answer for the last two hundred years.

When we think about the relative roles of competition and co-operation in creating successful economic systems, we have to distinguish between individuals and organizations. I think we all know that cooperation must be the guiding principle in relations between individuals. But economists believe that between organizations, particularly business enterprises, the best kind of relationship is competition, where each organization is trying to do as well as it can and, if possible, do better than its competitors in the market. An organization needs to be subject to an external challenge in order to perform well; otherwise it can so easily become lazy or corrupt.

These are two fundamentally different types of relationships. The founder of modern economic theory, Adam Smith, stressed the importance of both of them. Unfortunately, most subsequent economic theory has tended to overemphasize the importance of competition, and not only between organizations but between individuals as well. I think this is how economics got the name *the dismal science*. Of course there are different shades of opinion within economics, but in the last thirty years we have all been exposed to views promoting the idea that we need competition between individuals in the workplace, as well as between workplaces.

It's important to realize that economic theory is not a conspiracy; it's an idealistic intellectual exercise. The main proposition of economic theory is that free and competitive markets will produce the greatest possible happiness in the population, on one assumption: the only way people derive happiness is through the process of exchange in the marketplace. Of course, that theory has many limitations.

The problem is that so many of the things that are most important for human happiness come through relationships that are not conducted in the marketplace. They come through relationships in the family, or within the workplace between colleagues—which are not market relationships—or within the community, with your friends, or with people you meet in the street. These are also very important to your experience of a happy life.

We have neglected the aspect of human relationships too much for the sake of the increase in income and productivity in the competitive side of our lives. The result has been that we have experienced quite unparalleled increases in living standards and financial income, but this has not led to an increase in happiness. That's the paradox I want to discuss.

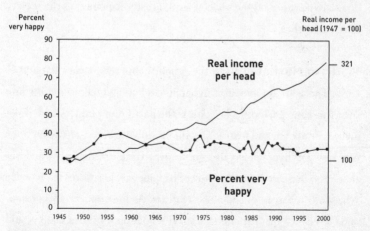

Figure 8.1: Real income per head measures the quantity of goods and services produced per head of a population, as a percentage of its 1947 value.

Here are the basic facts. In the United States of America, we see a huge increase in living standards in the post–World War II period from 1945 to 2000. Yet the percentage of people who say they're very happy is no higher than it was in the 1950s. The percentage of people who are not very happy is also the same.

Dalai Lama: From 1945 or 1950, just immediately after the war, the level of happiness is high while income is low. You see a lot of suffering or anxiety during the war, and immediately after it, more happiness. This might have to do with relief. Otherwise these numbers give the wrong impression, that when the economy is down and there is no growth, happiness spikes.

Richard Layard: We have similar data for Britain and West Germany, telling the same story. So the argument is that even in countries that are as rich as these ones have been since the war, you do not experience, at the societal level, greater happiness as the society becomes richer.

William Harbaugh: On the graph, happiness is very flat across time. There are no increases in happiness but big increases in income over this time period, right? This is the part I don't understand. Take away the income and instead put infant survival rates, or the number of years you live. Those also go up over time dramatically, and yet there's no increase in your report of happiness. This makes me wonder what your measure of happiness really is. As life expectancy goes up, and the chance that my children survive goes up, I'm sure that I would be happier, and yet your data doesn't show that.

Richard Layard: The measure is based on our asking people how happy they are. There are various questions: How happy are you with your life these days? How satisfied are you with your life these days? Now, you might say, "This is just something somebody says. Does it mean anything?" What is very encouraging is that if we each say how happy we are, and we each nominate a friend to report on how happy she thinks we are, what the friend says is very highly correlated with what we report about ourselves.

That's very reassuring. It would actually be very difficult for human society to operate if we couldn't see signs that told us about how happy another person was. I say that in order to counter skepticism about whether we can actually know how happy people are. Indeed, we also know, from Richie Davidson's work in particular, that we can identify brain activity that is correlated with how happy an individual says he is, both over time and across people. So we have to take the self-report very seriously.

Well, then, you say, "How can it be that people are giving these answers, and yet so much else is improving?" On life expectancy, I would like to make one important point. What I have been talking about has been the quality of life, a life lived at a particular time; the length of life is a separate question. There are many social scientists who think that the best measure of well-being in a country is the quality of life, per year lived, times the life expectancy.

Dalai Lama: Is there any real correlation between life expectancy and happiness? Of course, physical health is very much related to emotion, that's clear. Constant fear and constant anger shorten our life. But at the same time, a long life due to a healthy body and other faculties does not necessarily ensure that a person is mentally happy. I don't think so, but I don't know. These people are experts. They have research, I have no such thing.

William Harbaugh: Richard knows this better, but in general I think happiness does increase over one's life span. Age sixty-five or so is when it peaks, right?

Richard Layard: Yes. The conventional wisdom is that it goes down quite a bit up to about age forty-five, and then for most people, it starts to increase again.

Dalai Lama: Some of my friends once told me the modern world is so youth-oriented that getting older brings a feeling of uselessness. That's also possible. If the culture is very youth-oriented, then as you grow older, you may feel less and less relevant to society, and feel unproductive.

But basically I agree. Thirty, forty-five, fifty, you get deeper experience, and that experience brings, at least comparatively, a more holistic, wider perspective. And that helps to maintain more balance in our emotions. So on that I think I fully agree.

Richard Layard: Yes, but I think that what you say is correct, in particular in Western societies. From about seventy-five onward, then I start to have a decline because, as you know, we keep old people at arm's length within the family. We don't value them enough in the West.

There is an additional paradox here. Most individuals would like to be richer, and indeed what we find in a given society at a given point of time is that richer individuals are, on average, happier than poorer individuals. That may be a sad fact, but it is a fact. The data in one particular year for the United States shows how the groups that have higher income do have higher average happiness, though of course it flattens off at the top.

An individual becomes happier as he becomes richer, but over time the whole country does not become happier as it becomes richer. The explanation for this is that people compare themselves with other people. If somebody becomes richer, what is important to him is that he is becoming richer relative to all other people. This comparative wealth is important for the happiness of the individual.

But whenever someone's level of relative income goes up, someone

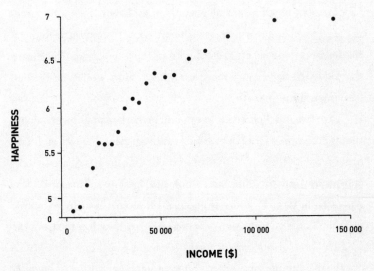

Figure 8.2.

else's has to go down. This is a very profound and important point, because it shows that the struggle to raise incomes is, to an important extent, fruitless. It cannot produce higher happiness. In technical language, we call this a *zero-sum game*. The total that can be achieved is fixed; all that can happen is that we rearrange who gets what from this total. To raise incomes is therefore not a meaningful overall goal for a society. Many social scientists now think that economic growth ought to no longer be the main goal for Western societies. This has begun to be an issue even at the political level, with [former] French president Nicolas Sarkozy, the Organisation for Economic Cooperation and Development (OECD), and others raising questions about the true meaning of "progress."

As we try to escape from the rat race of the zero-sum game, we have to refocus. If we want our societies not to be on the flat plain of happiness but moving onto a higher plain, we have to focus on sources of happiness that *can* be increased. Those come from positive-sum activities where each party is gaining from the interaction. This means that we have to give much more attention to human relationships and less to economic growth.

My strong belief is that economic growth simply means doing things better, and that commitment to progress will never end. I do not agree with the zero-growth approach. Of course we have to limit enormously our use of natural resources, but we will become cleverer and cleverer at doing things, and that will lead to economic growth. So the continuation of economic growth will come from the creative force of the human spirit. It's not a bad thing, but it's also not the most important thing. The most important thing is the quality of our human relationships, and we should not be sacrificing these relationships in order to further jack up the rate of economic growth, which is what has been happening in recent years.

For example, members of the financial community argued very strongly for less regulation of the financial system. The argument was that it would produce faster economic growth. This may or may not have been true in the long run, but the question was always what could be the cost? Anybody who thought about it should have known that the cost could be lower stability in the economic system. And what does low stability mean? It means greater likelihood of unemployment, of people losing their working relationships, which are one of the most important sources of human satisfaction. But whole groups of economists—especially at the University of Chicago—tried to persuade the rest of the profession that long-term economic growth was more important than the stability of the system and the avoidance of unemployment. This was a very shocking argument, but it was quite widely accepted.

Of course one could ask if the great economic success produced by competition is not so important for human happiness, why do we not consider other forms of economic organization? For example, should we consider a whole economic system that is based on cooperation? That, of course, was the Communist idea, that each part of the system should be engaged in a cooperative contribution to the public good.

What we find is that if you do not allow the free market, you do not allow many other freedoms as well. This is the fundamental problem with this argument, which produced a very unhappy society in the Communist world. As the graph shows, the former Communist countries were nearly all among the most unhappy countries ever

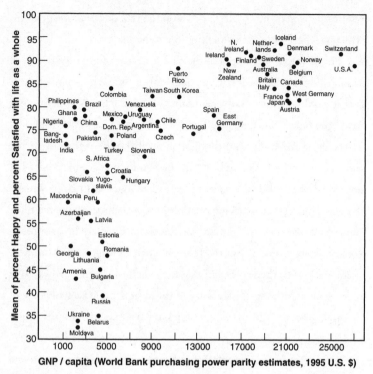

Figure 8.3.

recorded around the time Communism ended. Countries at similar income levels that were not Communist—what we might call developing countries—had higher happiness levels. Modern, advanced countries were happier still. There is a difference between the levels of happiness in the developing world and in the developed world, which is connected with the escape from absolute poverty. But when we get to the developed world, we come back to my original point that absolute poverty is not the issue. The issue now has become relative income levels within a society, and that is why economic growth isn't creating happiness growth and thus can't really be the main goal for modern society.

Dalai Lama: I have heard people say that when you compare the level of happiness between the people of Britain and the people of Cuba, the level of happiness is higher in Cuba. Why is that?

Richard Layard: Cuba is an interesting country, because the happiness level in Cuba is high relative to that of the typical country at that income level. I'm sure this is because of the more cooperative spirit that was established there, but of course there were also other limits coming from the absence of freedom.

Happiness has become a political issue that many countries around the world are considering. For example, in Britain, the government statistical office is considering regularly measuring the happiness of the population as an alternative to measuring the GDP, and this is happening in a lot of other countries too. It's an international movement.

But the question remains: if we want to raise the level of happiness, how do we do it? I think there are two key components. One is our relationship with others, and the other is our inner life. Both of these have to be present and fulfilling. When we talk about relationships between people, one of the key issues is trust. A very interesting question that has been asked in many countries over many years is, do you think most other people can be trusted? In the most trusting countries, which are in Scandinavia, nearly 70 percent of people say yes, but just within the sample of OECD countries, in some places,

like Portugal, it's as low as 10 percent. So there is a very wide variation. In Britain and America it used to be about 60 percent, and it's
now fallen to about 35 percent.

Dalai Lama: I think maybe we cannot generalize about Great
Britain, or about such and such a country. I think within a country
there is a difference between people in big cities and people in the
countryside, where there is a smaller population, where the way of
life is closer to nature, where people work in farming, for example.
Where you have a smaller nation, a smaller community, a smaller
number of people, I think personal relations may be stronger than in
a big city.

Richard Layard: That's an important factor, but I think that
ideology is also a very important factor. In the last thirty years there
has been a huge growth of individualism, and a belief that what is
right for the individual is to try to be as successful as possible compared
with other people. This has led many people to perceive others as a
threat rather than a source of support. So it's a mixture of the lifestyle
and beliefs about the goals of living that lead to differences in the
level of trust.

I'd like to end with some thoughts about how we can improve
trust and inner life. A factor that is very closely related with trust is
income equality. The countries with the greatest levels of trust, as
indeed of happiness, are the Nordic countries and the Netherlands.
These are also the most equal of the countries in the OECD in terms
of the distribution of income. The less equal the country, the lower
the level of trust.

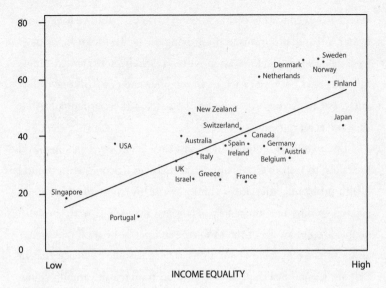

Figure 8.4.

There is obviously a relationship here, but I don't think that income distribution in itself is affecting trust. Rather I think both of these variables are being affected by the spirit of equality, and the strength of a community's view that people should respect each other as equals with equal rights to happiness. This is much more strongly entrenched in the Nordic countries than anywhere else in the Western world, and it has implications in many areas of life there.

The question is, how can we rebuild our societies on a stronger basis of mutual respect and mutual regard for the equal right of each person to happiness? I think that in social policy, schools are very, very important. We have to use our schools to create an ethos of mutual respect. In England we now have a group of schools providing values-based education that are trying to do this, and we have good, evidence-based programs for improving life skills. At work, we need to create a spirit of cooperation within teams by not trying to single out the contribution of each team member and pay each one differently, but by paying everyone on the basis of their group contribution and achievement.

I'm no expert on inner life, but I have been very much involved in trying to improve the support available for people with mental health problems, who are, I think, one of the most shockingly neglected groups in our society. They are neglected partly because people are not aware of the problem, and partly because they're not aware of the existence of solutions. There is some evidence that in Britain, mental health problems have been increasing among young people; but there is also evidence of the success rate of newer psychological therapies, which are scientifically evaluated and based on many ideas common in Buddhist thinking, about looking at yourself from the outside, understanding yourself, promoting the positive side of yourself, and so forth.

I just want to end with a new initiative I'm involved with, if I may. We are hoping to transform our culture through a mass movement called Action for Happiness, which we are launching in England quite shortly. Hopefully others will do it elsewhere, too. The idea is that we will have a manifesto where people commit themselves to trying to produce more happiness and less misery in the world, in all the things that they do in private and in public. They will sign the manifesto on the website and then be able to form groups of like-minded people. Of course, they will need support, so the website will have suggestions of dozens of things that a group can do to promote either their inner peace or the peace of the external society. There will also be a supporting structure of events and so on.

Dalai Lama: I think this is very, very encouraging. Up to now, people have simply stressed the importance of economic development, and all their mental energy and physical energy have been concentrated on it. Recently, when the Indian prime minister was in Washington, he said that where the economy is concerned, India is behind China, but India has other values: democracy, an independent judiciary, transparency, freedom of expression, free information. India has these values that are lacking in China. When I heard him drawing attention to these factors, I was very happy.

I think that now, for example, in the G7 or the G8 or the G20, everyone is focused on economic matters; nobody is paying attention to other values—happiness or satisfaction, individual freedom, genuine cooperation based on trust and respect. In my view, genuine cooperation is ultimately very much based on respecting others' rights and loving others.

I once met a Sufi practitioner who in our meeting said just these words: "I need you." I think the whole world needs that kind of concept now. I often tell people that we should eliminate the notion of "they." "We" should be enough; the whole world is part of we. This is not necessarily some kind of old-fashioned way of thinking, or an altruistic forgetting of one's own interests. I want happiness, so in order to achieve that, I need you. Economically, at every level, we need them. Once we develop that kind of feeling, that kind of view, then trust will come. First we extend our hand to the other. Sometimes their response may not be very positive; then we have the right to react accordingly. But expecting outreach from the other, without reaching out yourself first, that's wrong. We should take the initiative; then I think there's more chance of a positive response.

I really appreciate all our participants' focusing on the inner values. That's my main interest. Not just interest—I really feel that's the most important thing in building a happy world. Once you consider the other and respect the other, then there is no room for cheating, exploiting, or bullying, and then trust comes, and also competition in a good sense. I want to be equal to my friends, to those I hold dear, so that kind of positive competition is okay. Trying to hinder others or create obstacles in order to come in first, that's negative competition, isn't it? But positive competition, I think, is very good.

Ernst Fehr: I think the data Richard has shown us about comparing ourselves to others are really fundamentally important. We compare ourselves to others, to our friends, colleagues, and neighbors, and research has shown that if their income grows, then our happiness falls. That's a shocking fact.

At the root of this is social comparison; our happiness depends on the degree to which we are better off than others in material terms. And here is the challenge: this is even ingrained in our biology. Experimental data show that if Bill and I are engaging in a task and we are both successful, but for some reason I get $100 and Bill gets $50, my brain tells me that I'm happier than when I get $100 and Bill also gets $100. This is the social comparison process.

That means this is really in our biology, which tells us that if we want to make progress in this regard, we need to consider changing people. We need tools that change this desire to be better than others, this response of suffering when others succeed. This brings a whole new dimension, I believe, to the Buddhist enterprise. It's also a challenge for our schools. In addition to institutional changes, we should also think about how we could reorganize social life, and private life, to get rid of these detrimental social comparisons. I think this is not possible without a change in personality.

Gert Scobel: But you're not saying we change biology?

Ernst Fehr: Not everything in the brain is pure biology. What we see in the brain is very often a result of the experiences we have in social life. When I say "biology," I don't mean it's unchangeable, but it's something deep within our brains. If he's more successful than I am, then in my brain, I basically have a blip; my reward system shows less activity. That's something we have to change through practice, through education.

Dalai Lama: It makes sense, because the way you think would be reflected in the brain level. In my view, we place too much emphasis and importance on matter, or money. We believe money is the ultimate source of happiness. But if I value inner happiness, even if I am poor, my happiness may be better than that of a billionaire. The attitude of our whole society is to emphasize the value of material things too much, and never pay sufficient attention to inner values. I think that's a mistake. This work, and more discussion about these things, is helpful to create more awareness, to add more dimensions to the understanding of human happiness.

Usually we just focus on money, money, money—and power. Just that. If people get the idea that there are other sources of happiness, then they will pay more attention to those things. Then perhaps I think there's possibility for change. So I am very much impressed that you are not only just talking, but you are thinking about some kind of movement, some action. We need that. Thank you.

9

Why People Give to Charity

William Harbaugh

William Harbaugh is a professor of economics at the University of Oregon who studies why people make charitable donations. In his research, Bill uses methods ranging from economic theory to fMRI neuroimaging to show that the "warm-glow motive" is a powerful incentive to giving.

Bill's talk focused on the economic costs and the psychological benefits of charitable giving. Economists argue that even if giving is motivated by pure altruism, many people will simply do nothing, hoping that someone else will give so they won't have to. Bill argued that warm-glow altruism is an important alternate motive for giving that focuses on the benefits to the giver.

Modern economic systems are set up to operate in a way that increases happiness—maybe not perfectly, as Richard [Layard] has pointed out, but in general—particularly for the poor. In our current system, self-interest produces good results for society as a whole. The way it works is really quite simple. People can sell what they produce to another person, if that person values it more; and on the other hand, if they do something that harms another person, they have to pay. Those are the essential rules of the market capitalist system.

A central element in this system is the notion of price. Price does two things. First of all, it provides incentives to people. If you're a producer, the price is the amount of money that you get from the consumer, and you can take that price and turn it into something that you want. The price gives you an incentive to work hard, figure out a way to produce things more cheaply, and provide things people want. This is not nasty behavior; this is behavior that is good for people.

The other role that prices have in this market system is to provide information. When you are willing to pay a certain amount of money for something, then I know how much it's worth to you. That's important information to make society work. We need to know how much people value different things in order to structure the system in a way that increases everybody's happiness. The way that prices work is very interesting and complicated, but very beautiful. And the system that we have set up is very subtle and intentional. But there is a big "but" to this beautiful system, obviously, and that's why we're here today.

The truth is that price is not insular; its effects often spill over. Say you produce something, and the production process generates some pollution. That hurts other people, and sometimes the rules are set up so you don't have to compensate those other people. Economists call that an *externality*. The logic is very simple—if I don't have to pay for the damage I do to you, I can ignore it, and if I'm self-interested, I tend not to care about it either. The price doesn't provide me the incentive, and it doesn't provide me the information. I don't know how badly this hurt you if there's no price in the exchange.

It works the other way too. There are some important things, things that are very valuable for society, that just can't be produced without benefiting people who don't necessarily have to pay. There are a lot of examples of this, but I'm going to talk about one specific case here that I think will make the point.

The example is welfare, assistance, or other help for needy people in society. Most of us care about this. The well-being of the poor is not a market good that has a price attached to it; it's a public good. If I care about the poor and the well-being of the poor increases, I feel happier, even if it wasn't me who helped make the poor better off. So I can get that feeling of well-being without paying for it. I can hope that somebody else pays for it and still enjoy the benefits.

The result of this is that there's not enough support, not enough assistance, not enough help for low-income people in our own societies or for poor countries. Rich countries don't do enough to help poor countries; they hope somebody else will help. We need a solution to this. We have two choices: we can either rely on charitable gifts, or we can tax people and force them to pay to help support the poor.

Countries vary widely in how they deal with this issue. In the United States, 68 percent of families give something to charitable causes of all kinds, not just to those that help the poor but also to cultural and educational institutions and other organizations. There are a lot of people making charitable contributions, and they're giving about 2 percent of their income away. There are also big variations in that number across countries. In the United Kingdom, they give about 1 percent away; in France, 0.3 percent; and in Italy, 0.1 percent.

One reason we give so much in the United States is that there's not a lot of government help for poor people, unlike in Switzerland or the United Kingdom. My point here is not that one country is more generous than another, but that generosity takes different forms. There is also an interesting variation between giving at different income levels. The poor give a surprisingly large percentage of their income to help provide these goods—people with an annual income of less than $10,000 give away 5 percent of it. As people get richer, they give a smaller percentage—people with an income of $45,000 give an average of 1 percent. With incomes over $100,000, people give about 3 percent. The very wealthy give more and more and more, so it starts going back up.

Giving also increases with age, which may be related to happiness. Young people give about 2 percent; as people approach retirement, they give away more and more money to charity, about 4 percent. There is also a consistent correlation between education and generosity. The higher one's education, the greater percentage of income one gives.

Now I'll try to explain some of the variations. These are big differences—some associated with income, some with age, some with education. But even among people of the same age with the same education, some give very little, and some give a lot. We want to understand more deeply the roots of these variations.

To look at this question, I did an experiment with two colleagues at the University of Oregon: Ulrich Mayr, a psychologist, and Daniel Burghart, an economist. In the experiment, we give people $100, and they can keep it or give some of the money to a food bank that buys food to give to low-income people. So it's a very simple charitable contribution: I give up some money, and somebody who's less well off than I am gets a basic necessity.

The trick in this experiment is that we change the price of giving. Sometimes we make it very cheap to give money away to the charity: I give away $15, and the food bank receives $45. But sometimes it's very expensive: to give $15 to the charity, I would have to give up $45. We have everyone make a lot of these choices, telling them that we will pick one at random to count for real money. And we follow through—if the subject agrees to give in that condition, we take the money from their payment, and we mail a check to the charity. They can even watch us mail it if they want.

Then we take the data and do very simple economic modeling; we could call this the *altruistic supply function*. It's similar to the demand function for a commodity like shoes. As the price of shoes goes up, people buy fewer shoes. Likewise, as it gets more expensive to make a charitable contribution, people donate less often and give smaller amounts.

For an economist, this is a nice model. We estimate functions like this constantly, and when they look like that—it gets more expensive, so people do less of it—we think that people are making a rational decision. They're comparing the benefit that poor people would get with the cost to themselves. When the benefit is very high and the cost is very low, people can be extremely altruistic: 80 percent of people give some money in those circumstances. But when the cost is very high, people say, "No, I'll keep the money for myself now." That's a rational cost-benefit calculation. You would have to be very altruistic indeed to give away everything when it costs you a great deal and does little to benefit others.

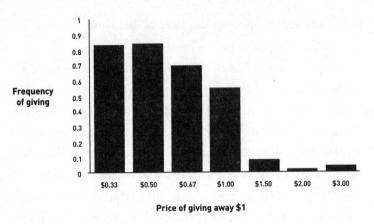

Figure 9.1.

But we're still left with the question of why people care about the benefit to others. That is a bit of a mystery. So there's more to the experiment that tries to get at the question of why. In the experiment, we don't just give people a chance to make giving decisions; we also add in a tax component. Just like in the real world, we tax the subjects, and we give the money to the charity. There's no choice in this part of the design, just like there's no choice with real taxes. We tell them, "I'm going to take $15 from you and give it to poor people, end of story." The giving and the taxation parts are repeated in random order, and just as with the giving, one round is randomly chosen to count in reality, with the respective amounts given to the charity and to the participant.

Normally you can't study economics if you aren't asking people to make a choice, because you don't see any behavior. But what we do here is have them pay this tax while they're inside an fMRI scanner. They don't make a choice, but we can see what happens to their brain activity as we take their money away and give it to the charity.

The region of the brain called the *ventral striatum* is very important to processing rewards of all kinds. For example, if you gave an animal sweet food, this part of the brain would light up. In our experiment, when the subject gets more money for herself or pays less in taxes, the activation in this reward area increases. There's a pleasurable reaction from getting money for yourself. Other areas are activated when money goes to the charity, to help other people. The important thing to notice is that there's a lot of overlap between these areas, activated when you get money; they also activate when you see the charity get money. This means that the inputs that help you make the decision of whether or not to give are coming from nearby and sometimes identical regions of the brain.

There is another reason I tend to believe that people make rational decisions about charitable giving. It turns out that we can actually predict decisions in the voluntary giving parts of the experiment based on the relative magnitude of the brain activation in these regions and other closely related regions during the mandatory taxation parts of the experiment. The people who show larger rewards in these areas when the charity gets money and smaller rewards when they get money for themselves are significantly more likely to give away money during the voluntary giving part of the experiment than those who show the reverse pattern of activation (controlling for the cost of the giving).

There's a catch to all of this. It's a very nice story so far, but we still have to worry about self-interest. Our experiment shows that people who experience more reward activation from seeing the charity get money are more likely to give, but in the real world this motive is very easily wiped out by the free riding effect. In other words, I may genuinely care about the well-being of the poor but still not contribute much to help them because I believe that donations from other people or government aid are addressing part of the need. My contributions might still be valuable to others, but I judge them not worth the cost to me. This creates the problem that people are not going to provide enough public goods.

Thus, while the sort of pure altruism we measure is very nice, it cannot lead to meaningful increases in charitable giving in a large economy. Most people still hold back. With just two people, it's no problem. If I care about the other person and nobody else is available to help, I'll help him. But in a large economy there are thousands of people who might help; when that's the case, even though I care about this person, I also care about myself, and so I hope that Richard will help him instead of me having to. Everyone thinks that way. So pure altruism can be a strong emotion, but it might not lead to big behavior.

Depressing news, right? But there's a solution. There's an alternative kind of altruism that might solve this problem. Economists call it *warm-glow altruism*. The name comes from the economist Jim Andreoni. Warm-glow altruism is more egoistic than pure altruism, so economists sometimes call it "impure altruism." It comes from the good feeling that you get from knowing that *you're* the person who helped the poor—not someone else, not the government, but you. This may not be pure, but it's more effective, because here I can only get that good feeling if I contribute personally. If somebody's poor and other people are helping him, I still want to help him more in order to get this good feeling for myself. We have found evidence of this warm-glow feeling in our experiment. The reward area activation is, on average, significantly stronger when people voluntarily give money than when they are taxed. People seem to get an extra neural benefit from making the decision to help others and the contribution voluntarily.

It is striking that the reward areas in the ventral striatum are part of the same general brain system that is central to learning. Certain actions, like eating sweet foods, activate these areas, so we learn to seek out sweets. Now, I doubt anyone is born having an innately pleasurable reaction to money. Instead we learn that money can buy things that activate our brain's reward system, and the brain starts to react to the money in response. This suggests that people can learn that they can get a neural warm-glow benefit from giving money away. This learning might lead us to seek out opportunities to give, leading to a more altruistic society.

The conclusion is that when it comes to providing for the needy in society, we can rely on the market sometimes, but we also need to rely on altruism. The question is, what kind of altruism will get us to a world where things like welfare for the poor are provided? In a world with so many diverse peoples and countries, I believe pure altruism is not enough. Instead we should cultivate this warm-glow form of altruistic feelings.

Dalai Lama: "Warm-glow." From a Buddhist psychology viewpoint, even when we talk about one mental phenomenon like altruism, it seems that there are so many different degrees and types. This research work is wonderful.

William Harbaugh: Thank you. After hearing about the work of the people gathered here, I think that Buddhism can offer many ideas on how to cultivate this warm-glow kind of altruism. I'm very optimistic.

Altruistic Punishment and the Creation of Public Goods

Ernst Fehr

Previous presentations have shown compelling evidence that altruism does exist. Ernst extended the discussion to ask why altruism matters and how it can solve social problems. Public goods are crucial to high-functioning societies, he argues, and they can be created and sustained in environments that pair opportunities for altruistic punishment with strong civic norms.

During our conversations here, we have seen a lot of evidence that the old view that people are self-interested and don't care for others is wrong. This has been shown through powerful behavioral evidence, and through neural evidence. We have seen that when people act for selfish gains, reward areas in their brains are activated, and that these same reward areas are activated when people engage in pro-social, altruistic activities, providing hope that we can cultivate altruism even further. People will always have some self-interested desires, but we now know that altruistic concerns can create powerful motivation as well.

Thus my question is not whether altruism exists, but what it can do for us. I want to explore the implications of altruism in generating human welfare, which depends in substantial ways on the provision of public goods. Let me repeat the definition of a public good from an economist's standpoint, because it is perhaps not the same as what one would think from a layman's perspective. We say a public good exists for a social group if it can be consumed by all members of the group, regardless of their contribution to the financing of the good. Welfare for the poor is one example. If Bill [Harbaugh] relieves poverty and I care about poverty, Bill's action is also good for me. But as Bill discussed in the last presentation, this generates a big problem: those who do not contribute to the good also benefit from it, so there is a free riding incentive. In addition, those who contribute to the public good bear the cost and bring advantages to others, implying that contribution to a public good is an altruistic act. I incur a cost that brings a benefit to other people.

Now, based on this definition, you see immediately that selfish people will generally free ride. They want others to produce, and they want to consume. Selfish people will rarely produce sufficient public goods, which is at the core of the problem. Let me give a few examples of important public goods, because the definition I've given so far is quite abstract. I think one of the most important public goods—and it's not generally recognized to be one—is democratic liberties for all citizens. Fights against dictatorships are costly for individuals. Look at the recent conflicts in Iran and all over the Middle East. Tibet is also an example, and so is the history of Europe.

All the people who were at Tiananmen Square in 1989 fought

for democratic liberties, and they had a huge price to pay. They did not succeed in that case, but in many other countries, in the long run, people succeeded in establishing democratic liberties. Once they are established, everybody benefits, even those who did not contribute to the creation of that public good.

Other more obvious public goods are avoiding global warming, preventing the overfishing of the sea, and the supply of clean air. Another public good that has played a particularly important role in recent times is good corporate governance. Many of us are probably outraged by income inequality within companies, when CEOs are paid a lot of money that the general public sometimes feels is not deserved. This is a public goods problem from the shareholders' viewpoint. If I am a shareholder in a large company and contribute to the control and efficient functioning of the management, to keep the management responsible, I incur a huge cost. It's more than a full-time job, but all shareholders would benefit.

The core of the problem, one of the biggest social problems in the world, I think, is that there is an undersupply of public goods if people behave in a selfish manner. That's where human altruism comes in. How can we get a grip on this problem? How can we study it in a direct way?

One way is to set up an experiment. The experiment goes as follows. I take a group of ten people to my laboratory and give each of them $10. They can keep the $10 for themselves, or they can contribute it to a project with the following characteristics: If I'm a group member and I spend $1 on the project, the experimenter doubles the amount. Now there is $2 in the project, and the experimenter distributes the $2 equally among the people in the group.

You can immediately see the incentive structure here. If I

contribute $1, the experimenter doubles it and it becomes $2. This is divided by ten, which gives me 20¢ back. So I spend $1 and get 20¢ back. From a selfish viewpoint, I shouldn't do this. However, for the group as a whole it's beneficial, because the group as a whole gets $2, and I spent only $1. If all of us spent our $10 on the public good, we would all double our incomes, but we have this free riding incentive. If I consider only my own welfare, I would never contribute.

This is how we conduct the experiment: People stay together for ten periods and interact with each other while still maintaining their anonymity. The group members interact with the help of computer terminals so that they never know the personal identity of the other group members. In period one, they decide how much to contribute to the public good simultaneously. At the end of the period, they get feedback about what everybody else did. Then they get another $10, and they can decide whether to contribute or not, for ten periods.

What do we observe in the results? Participants do pretty well in period one. Between periods one and two, they spend between 40 and 60 percent of their income on the public good. This is a sign of altruism. However, when they play for ten periods, the cooperation rate plummets. And this happens not just in Zurich, where we ran the experiment originally. This is almost a universally observed phenomenon. My colleague Simon Gächter ran this experiment in fifteen different countries, and he observed this same pattern in all of them.

Dalai Lama: Why is there a huge spike at the beginning? Is it because of the novelty factor, or curiosity, or excitement?

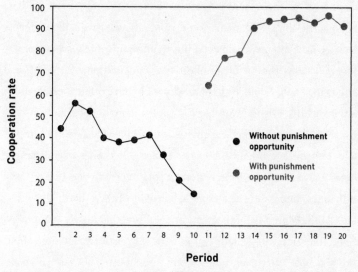

Figure 10.1: Participants can contribute to the public good over ten periods. At the end of each period, they find out how much the other participants contributed in that period. Then they may use that information to make their contribution decision in the next period.

When the public goods experiment is conducted without sanctioning opportunities, contributions strongly decline over the ten periods. When the experimenter introduces the possibility of sanctioning, contributions to the public good rise rapidly to almost 100 percent by period twenty.

Ernst Fehr: That's an interesting question. It's really a puzzle. As many people here have told you, people are altruistic. If you look at period ten, altruism is pretty meager. But if you look at period one, it's not so bad. So is the glass half full or half empty? Are people altruistic or not? Why is this happening?

Here's what we know so far. In this data set, we have roughly 50 percent of people who contribute more to the public good the more they believe that others contribute. We call them *conditional cooperators*. Then we have 30 percent who contribute zero, regardless of what they believe the others contribute. So we have selfish subjects and we have altruistic subjects, but their altruism takes a particular form. It takes the form of conditional cooperation, or conditional altruism. I behave more altruistically if I believe others behave more altruistically. On the one hand, that's a very hopeful notion, because that means if I behave altruistically, I provide a good example, and I encourage others to do the same. But there's also a danger here, because the self-interested people depress everything; their selfishness depresses the altruistic behavior of the others.

At the beginning of the experiment—and this answers your question, Your Holiness—many people have optimistic expectations about other people's altruism, but they are disappointed because there are consistent free riders. When they see the others free ride, they don't want to continue to feed the free riders, so they stop cooperating. Over time, almost everyone stops cooperating. We have conducted experiments where literally, in period ten, nobody cooperates anymore. Cooperation is zero.

How can we solve that problem? Before I go to that question, let me also point out how important I think the conditionality of altruism is. Think, for example, of the issue of illegitimate consumption of benefits provided by the welfare state. The wider the belief that welfare benefits are drawn illegitimately, the greater the individual readiness to do so as well. If you don't monitor the eligibility of those who request welfare benefits, then more and more people start exploiting the welfare state, claiming benefits even if they don't qualify for them. The same happens with regard to corruption. The more corrupt the society is as a whole, the more each individual is willing to engage in corrupt acts. The more criminality we observe, the more each individual, on average, is likely to be willing to engage in criminal acts. Thus this conditionality is hugely important. It implies that a task for policy makers, for CEOs, for everybody in society in a sense, is to contribute to the expectation that we cooperate, because that in itself generates cooperation.

However, as we have seen, this is not enough. The expectation itself breaks down if you don't have supporting institutions that somehow constrain free riding. How did we solve this historically? We did it by sanctioning noncooperation. We sanctioned the people who exploited the welfare state; we sanctioned the criminal; we sanctioned the people who didn't pay their taxes; and so on. However, the institutions that help maintain cooperation, like the rule of law, democracy, impartial police and independent judges, contract law, taxation—all these institutions have come up in the last millisecond of human history. For 99 percent of our history, we had to do without them. And this raises a very important question and puzzle: how have humans been able to create such institutions, which are themselves public goods?

I want to provide you with the partial answer, based on experiments we have done at the University of Zurich. We conducted the same public goods experiment as before, but we added a sanctioning opportunity. In each period, people first make a contribution decision. Then they are informed on a computer screen about the contributions of the other individuals in the group. They see what others did, and then they can use their money to sanction others. For every $1 a person spends on sanctioning, the income of the sanctioned group member is reduced by $3. You would think that this is an idiotic thing to do. Why should anyone do this? But the people in the experiment immediately grasped that this was a sanctioning possibility, and they targeted their sanctions toward the free riders. For example, it was possible to assign a high sanction to a group member who contributed little or nothing to the public good, and a lower sanction (or no sanction) to a group member who contributed half of his income. You can easily see what the impact of that is. It should discipline the potential free riders, because they now face what economists or game theorists call a *credible threat*. Let us see what this altruistic sanctioning does.

Without sanctioning opportunities, cooperation totally broke down by period ten. In period eleven, I gave people the opportunity to sanction each other. It's amazing what happened. The same people who contributed literally zero in period ten contributed almost 100 percent—nearly all of their money—to the public good in period twenty. Isn't it amazing? The very same people. In a sense, you could view this experiment as a parable of human evolution. We have been able to provide essential public goods in the absence of a state, in the absence of a cooperative infrastructure like the rule of law, because we had an altruistic tendency to discipline those who did not live up to the rules of society.

And now the question is, is this a universal recipe? I told you before that the unraveling of cooperation seems to be a universal feature that is observed in every country where researchers have conducted this experiment. But as it turns out, the effectiveness of sanctioning is not universal. Punishment alone does not make all groups universally better off. The reason is that we see societies in which those who are punished strike back. Let's say I get punished by Bill in period fourteen because I did not contribute. This makes me angry, and I reason that it must have been one of these cooperators who punished me. I want to teach them a lesson, so in period fifteen, I single out one of them. This is an anonymous experiment. I don't know that I'm singling out Bill; I just take blind revenge on some cooperators in the next period. This is called *antisocial punishment*, and in some cultures it's really prevalent.

Benedikt Herrmann, Christian Thöni, and Simon Gächter[1] observed a lot of antisocial punishment in many countries, such as Greece and some places in the Middle East, whereas in countries like Switzerland or the U.S. they observed mainly pro-social altruistic punishment. When they looked at what is behind this difference, they observed that countries with strong civic norms have very little antisocial punishment. An example of civic norms is when people think it is wrong to use public transport without paying. This tells us that punishment alone is not doing the job. We need the right social norms, the right education. Then, in combination with sanctioning opportunities, we can generate valuable public goods. Cultures that have succeeded in establishing these norms have been able to contribute a lot to human welfare, because they have solved the public goods problem more successfully.

I argued that public goods are decisive for human welfare, that voluntary provision of public goods requires altruism, and that many people display altruistic cooperation, but this alone is not sufficient. Why? Because a small group of selfish individuals can destroy widespread altruistic cooperation. But many people also display a tendency for altruistic sanctioning, and even a small group of altruistic sanctioners can establish full cooperation if a group has the right cultural norms—which again reveals the importance of education, and enterprises like this conference.

One of the main lessons here is that the very same people can produce a disastrous outcome or a good outcome. It depends very much on how we design our institutions, and which action opportunities we establish. That's what is happening right now in the regulation of financial markets. It's all about the rules of the game. How can we constrain greed and self-interest in a way that it is not detrimental for society? Economics is sometimes called the dismal science, but in a sense it's a very noble science. It can enable us to design institutions that improve human welfare.

PART III

Introducing Pro-Sociality into Economic Systems

Profit with a Purpose

Antoinette Hunziker-Ebneter

Antoinette Hunziker-Ebneter is CEO and founding partner of Forma Futura Invest Inc., an independent asset management company focusing on investment opportunities that incorporate good governance and social and environmental responsibility. Earlier in her career, she headed the Swiss stock exchange and was chief executive officer of Virt-x, the first pan-European stock exchange.

Antoinette showed how investing in the right kinds of companies can promote social and environmental well-being while still producing a financial profit. When we use our money to create this kind of responsible profit, she said, large groups of people—from workers to management to investors—can mutually participate in the creation of a better quality of life for humans and better health for the planet.

Money is a vital resource, a cycle like water or knowledge. It has to flow. Cycles are the basis of sustainability, so it's very important that people who have money think and reflect before they invest. What kind of management, people, products, services, and production processes do we want to invest in, financially, socially, and ethically?

We are responsible for the current financial system we have. We are responsible for the economic system we have. These systems produce a lot of financial bubbles, and will continue to do so. Who is really profiting from those bubbles? It's a small group of very greedy people. Meanwhile, most other people are losing not only money, but also jobs and quality of life.

We are all participants in that system. We have to ask ourselves: are we allowed to stay ignorant? In order for us to participate responsibly, we have to share knowledge. If we analyze today's economic system, we see that its values are material growth, profit maximization, efficiency, short termism, individualism, and linear thinking. Are these really our values as consumers and investors? Less and less, I think. I see clients who really care where they invest. We are seeing a shift from profit to profit with a purpose, from quantity to quality of life; immaterial values are becoming more and more important.

Let's look at the pyramid of the financial needs of human beings. First, you need to be able to cover your basic needs: food, drink, shelter, education. Then you need to have some reserves, some financial security, for days when you are ill, for example. When you earn a bit more money, you might like to spend it on recreational activities, on sports and the arts. Finally, you also want to make a profit.

If you have been able to achieve those three levels, and you are aware of the impact of your investments, then you have the opportunity to take responsibility for your investments and use your money so that it can contribute to a better quality of life.

At our company, we analyze organizations according to 180 sus-

Figure 11.1: In the future, money must offer investors more than just the fulfillment of financial requirements or the realization of a profit.

tainability factors. Looking at the management, who leads the companies? What values do they stand for? If they communicate something, do they really do it? What are the incentive schemes? Are they long-term oriented? There are companies that set sustainability goals, for example, to issue less carbon dioxide every year, and combine that goal with an incentive scheme. At the investment bank where I worked before founding Forma Futura, I introduced an incentive scheme where bonuses were dependent upon our traders' embracing our values. For example, one of our key values was being fair to the client. So I measured the margin—that is, what the bank earned from selling the clients financial products and securities—and if our traders took too much, they got smaller bonuses. As you can imagine, within three to six months of implementing this policy, we saw a change in behavior in people. When we are fair with our clients, we can build up long-term relationships with them and convince them more and more to invest responsibly.

At Forma Futura, we also measure how companies foster innovation. I imagine that my seventeen-year-old son will someday live in a world where cars are no longer powered by fossil fuels, but that depends on what happens in the transportation sector in the next few years regarding innovation. Innovation needs a certain climate; it needs platforms. It requires combining the expertise of people from different fields and backgrounds.

We also measure how much greenhouse gas companies emit, how they handle scarce resources, if they have products for underserved markets, and how seriously they take human rights in their labor, production, and sourcing practices. After having done this sustainability analysis, we also do a conventional financial analysis. Investors can only invest in companies that have passed all these tests.

What we have been able to show over the last three and a half years is that you can earn at least as much money in these markets as if you invest in conventional models. Now we're also seeing that sustainable companies can get capital on the capital market cheaper than other companies, probably because those companies care more about risks and communicate that to the outside world.

Today in Europe, 3 percent of all money invested is invested in a sustainable way; in the United States it's about 10 percent. My personal goal is that I'm still alive when it's 25 percent, and that I can contribute to this development, together with my partners and employees and clients, so that the heads of companies can no longer ignore social and ecological factors.

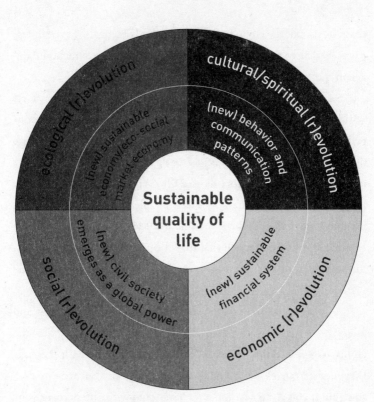

Figure 11.2: The transformation toward a sustainable quality of life is contingent upon four global (r)evolutions.

Changing the way we invest will be a major step in the right direction, but that alone won't create the comprehensive ethical and sustainable solution we need. What else can we be doing? I think we need four parallel global evolutions, or revolutions, or both. I'm personally more the type for evolution, but given what we've seen so far from the financial crisis, I doubt that it will be possible to do what needs to be done in an evolutionary way.

First, we need an ecological (r)evolution and a market economy that cares about the environment. If somebody is emitting greenhouse gases, he has to pay for it. We need to include environmental damage in our pricing models.

Second, we need a sustainable financial system, and this starts with setting reasonable goals. What kind of targets do we set in our economic system? We measure the GDP, but does the GDP increase quality of life? Only to a point, as we've seen. We measure the days of illness, and see that more days of illness increase the GDP. But in Bhutan, they are measuring the days people are healthy. They have invented what they call the *gross national happiness index*. We have to move more and more in that direction, setting reasonable goals for ourselves, our communities, our companies, and our economic system.

A sustainable financial system also needs a mandatory and effective regulatory framework. A very important factor is the equity-to-assets-ratio—banks should be able to cope with the risks they incur. Your Holiness, I don't know if you've ever been in a casino, but if you go to a casino, you have to go with 100 percent your own capital. Some of the business investments banks have been making are pure speculation. They should do that with their own money—this is also a kind of gambling—but in recent years they have been able to pressure regulatory bodies and decrease those quotas. Since the financial crisis, some banks have increased those quotas again, but it's not enough.

A sustainable financial system allows and requires responsibility. In large corporations, one of the tasks of board members is to find out about risks. They have to really ask about where these risks can arise and how they are going to be tackled. If you don't understand something, then you shouldn't do it.

Personally, I don't expect that kind of change to be instigated by our current corporate representatives. The real change will come, I believe, from social evolution or revolution, where we, civil society, will act in a responsible way. It's up to us to reflect and to decide what goods we will consume and how much of them. The new luxury goods aren't physical things; they are security, an intact ecosystem, friendships, happiness, and a meaningful life.

Of course, you also need a cultural and spiritual evolution, but that's your field of expertise, Your Holiness, so I'm really looking forward to seeing what else you will do in that sector in the future. With your support, we finally can move to a sustainable quality of life.

Dalai Lama: Wonderful. It's wonderful that there is a growing recognition of the shortcomings of the current status quo and existing system. There needs to be some change introduced.

I believe that we human beings, when our intelligence is used properly and we see things more holistically, have the ability to find ways and means to overcome these problems. Although we may not achieve it in our lifetime, it doesn't matter; we have to think, to investigate these things and make them clear to younger generations, who eventually will carry them out.

Gert Scobel: When you said that your investments have to make profit as well as any other product you buy or sell, what's really the difference? Because for me as a consumer, it's very difficult to know firsthand the difference between profit with a purpose and just plain profit. Is it that you think in terms of a longer period of time?

Antoinette Hunziker-Ebneter: Yes. Medium-sized companies in Switzerland, Germany, and elsewhere have always worked like that. For example, if there is a period of reduced earnings, first the owners of the company earn less; they don't just let people go or put them on furlough. That long-term thinking is fruitful in building know-how, in building trust, in building real loyalty. If you want people to do their best work, to really innovate and give their ideas to you, then you have to ensure that they can work with a sense of trust. If they are afraid, like so many people are right now, that they may lose their jobs at any time, you will not get their insights. So sustainable profit is profit that is long-term oriented; there will be periods without a lot of growth, like in nature. Trees don't grow endlessly, and this has to be accepted. If the company has a long-term view, and the investors don't ask for double-digit yields every year, then this is possible. So it depends a lot on the consumer as well.

Gert Scobel: So you are saying you will have profit? It might not be so huge at the beginning, but in the long run it is a constant.

Antoinette Hunziker-Ebneter: Yes, this gives companies time to work toward real solutions to current environmental challenges. For example, in energy efficiency, a company can say, "By 2015, 50 percent of our turnover will come from green products, products that save energy." Not only do they offer something very meaningful, but investors can also participate in that growth. Or there are companies that develop enzymes that enable you to do laundry at lower temperatures. We need this kind of holistic view of the economic, social, and ecological world of one product. This integrated way of management leads to profit, which is a good thing. We need to make a reasonable profit to be able to pay our employees and ourselves, and of course for innovation.

Dalai Lama: It's important to remember there are limitations. I tell people that when material development is concerned, there are always limitations, so in that field it's better to practice contentment. With mental development, there's no limitation, so it's better not to have contentment there and instead try to further develop, further develop, further develop. But usually we do just the opposite. The mental development, nobody pays much attention to it. But on the material side, even if there are limitations, all our hope is put into seeing if we can go past the limit.

I really appreciated your comment about the need to recognize that there's going to be limits to the growth. This is something I really believe, and of course it's very human to feel delighted when you find someone who shares the same kind of deep idea with you.

12

What Can Microfinance Do?

Arthur Vayloyan

Arthur Vayloyan held various executive positions at Credit Suisse from 1992 to 2012. He is a former member of the organization's Private Banking Management Committee, and most recently served as head of the Private Banking Switzerland and Global External Asset Managers divisions. He is particularly interested in nanotechnology, innovation, and microfinance.

Arthur narrated the history and significance of Credit Suisse's engagement in microfinance, which has created an efficient, profitable, and sustainable way to bring the money of the world's top economic earners to people who can use it to rise out of poverty. Later, Antoinette, Matthieu, and His Holiness discussed the possibilities and risks of big banks joining the microfinance movement.

Thank you, Your Holiness, ladies and gentlemen; what an opportunity. When we talk about big banks and big companies, when we read the headlines, we tend to forget that within those big entities are human beings who do care. At the beginning of this millennium, some people at our bank, Credit Suisse, began to think about what we could do to help this world progress, to meaningfully support the reduction of poverty. One thing we tend to forget when we talk about poverty is the crucial role of access to financial services. We take it for granted; for us it's normal. But billions of people lack that access.

Initially the reaction at Credit Suisse was, "Forget it; this is not our job." So the small group of people promoting this had to think, is there a meaningful way to link the natural activities of a bank with billions of people who are in need? Around this time, microfinance happened to become well known, so we said, why shouldn't we try it? A debate started. One of the arguments was that there was no need for us to do this, because the world was getting better. In 1980, the world's population was 4.4 billion; in 1990, 5.3 billion; in 2000, 6 billion; and very soon it will be more than 7 billion people.[1] Rather unexpectedly, the level of extreme poverty decreased in that time period, from 1.9 billion people living below the poverty line in 1980, which was more than 40 percent of the global population, down to around 20 percent today.

Extreme poverty is decreasing in general terms. But there are huge regional differences, and there are still millions of children and adults in this world who are in despair. Child mortality in Angola is 18 percent. The illiteracy rate in Burkina Faso is 76 percent. Income per capita per day in Mozambique is $2. Life expectancy in Swaziland is age thirty-two. I have picked numbers here from Africa, but we can easily find these kinds of statistics for other parts of the world too. And despite the need, we see aid flattening out. So to relax and say the world will take care of itself is a cheap answer.

We see more and more migration, because people need to move from a poor place to a place where they can have a better life. An-

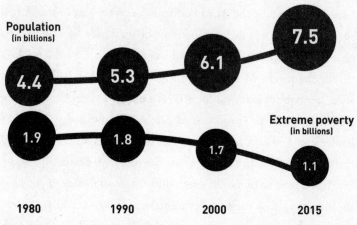

Figure 12.1.

other issue we should definitely care about is youth bulge, or the share of young people within a society. In the developed world, young people between fifteen and twenty-five years old are a small fraction of the population, around 10 percent. In the developing world, there is a huge proportion of young people with no future; and as we know, young people without a future can fall victim to all sorts of violent ideologies.

So do we really need microfinance? First we need to understand what it is. To give a very quick summary, it's actually nothing more than financial services: credit, payments, savings, and insurance. Normally when people talk about microfinance they are talking about microcredit, but actually microfinance includes all the classical finance activities.

Here's one example out of millions: Phi Phi, a mother of four who lives in a village in Cambodia. This is a woman who had no money at all. Her first loan was for just $13. That helped her kick-start a new business. Previously she'd had a difficult carpentry business, and then she made a shift to sugar production. She used her first loan to purchase a few sacks of fertilizer and some bamboo for ladders. As a result, she produced more palm sugar per day than before. Years later, her twelfth loan was for $65; she used it to acquire one more plot of land and to enroll one of her sons in university. Phi Phi's lender was Amret, a microfinance institution in Cambodia that receives capital from the Credit Suisse microfinance fund.

If you have no money, it's very difficult to get money. If you have some money, it's actually easier to make it grow—if you are an entrepreneur and you have a business idea. How could a woman such as Phi Phi qualify for her first loan? That is where sometimes people get a bit too romantic when they talk about microfinance. People still have to apply for and qualify to get microcredit, and there are penalties for default and rewards for repayment. In fact, Phi Phi could only get access to money because she was part of a group. That's why it is sometimes called *village banking* or *solidarity banking*. She wouldn't have qualified alone, but as a member of a group she could.

One thing you will note about this story: the beneficiary is a woman, and that's not by accident. Many microfinance products specifically target women because they tend to show higher repayment rates for loans than men do, and because women often bear the responsibility for the well-being of the whole family. That's why it's no surprise that a large majority of microentrepreneurs, when they are starting from zero and building something up, are groups of women. Phi Phi started with her small loan and had some success. There was a group supporting her—there was the microfinance institution, a credit officer helping her—and she could build up more and more business, more and more money. The very moment she can repay her loan, she builds up trust, and it's exactly that trust capital that makes her qualify for more and more loans. But we also have to remember that money itself is not the goal. Phi Phi's goal was to see her children go to school, to have access to quality health care, to have a house, to have a decent life relative to where she started.

Today—as we speak here—there are 155 million microcredit clients in the world. A staggering $45 billion in credit has been dispersed globally. These numbers reflect all the participants in the market, not just our bank. But we cannot stand still and say, "That's great; we have achieved something." The potential number of clients is over tenfold where we are now, so we cannot stop. According to estimates, 2.5 billion of the world's adults don't use banks or microfinance institutions to save or borrow money.[2]

Aid alone will not do the job, and this is where we think our bank can have a meaningful contribution. We serve people at the top of the wealth pyramid: some 10 million people, out of over 6.5 billion, who have financial assets of $1 million or more. The bottom of the pyramid is huge: 4.5 billion people with less than $4 a day in purchasing power parity who need access to capital. If we can bring the fortune at the top to the bottom in a sustainable, long-term way, we can accelerate development.

How do you do this in practice? We know it doesn't work to just take money and say, "I have some money; who needs money?" At our bank we realized we need a simple solution that we can offer to our clients and to anyone who is interested in being a part of it. The idea was to find investors who would understand and support the idea, and who would put money into what we call a *microfinance fund*. That microfinance money is given to microfinance institutions, banks, or quasi-banks in over thirty-five countries from east to west, north to south. Those microfinance institutions then give out loans to microentrepreneurs, like the $13 to Phi Phi. Investments in the fund earn interest; Credit Suisse's financing of the microfinance institutions bears interest; and the client repays the loan principal plus interest to the microfinance institution. That's how it works.

When I first presented this idea to the Credit Suisse executive board, one of the members asked why I was wasting their time. In part this was because initially the fund was very small. After contemplating how we should do it, we finally started. At the end of 2003, we began the venture with $4 million in money from friends and family—people who really believed in us, who trusted us, who thought it was an idea worth investing in. Since then it has evolved dramatically. Only a year later it had increased tenfold, another year later it had increased fivefold, and today we're almost up to a billion dollars. A billion dollars invested means that hundreds of thousands of microentrepreneurs have a better life, and we don't see an end to that growth in sight.

Somewhat counterintuitively, unexpectedly, the global financial crisis did not damage the evolution of this investment idea. The reason is that microentrepreneurs are not linked in any way to the top of the economic pyramid that Antoinette showed us,[3] where people have all their financial needs met and can be choosy about where they invest their money.

Of course, microfinance is not the solution for everything. The best way to describe it is as a catalyst, a little thing that can have huge

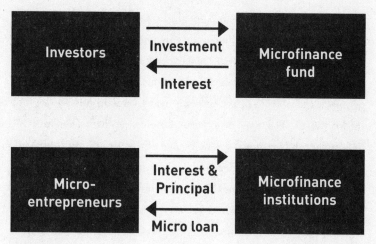

Figure 12.2.

impact. Initially nobody believed it could work, but it has grown and will continue to grow. Let me finish by quoting Nelson Mandela, who said, "It always seems impossible until it's done." Thank you.

Dalai Lama: A microfinance investment makes money, but purely from the point of view of investment returns, if you compare it with conventional investment, how does it perform?

Arthur Vayloyan: It obviously cannot be in the high 20 percent range, and it doesn't aspire to be there. We think of it like this: If you put money in a bank account, you get almost nothing nowadays. If you put money in this fund, you get a couple percent in returns. This fund returned almost 6 percent in 2009; it was a fabulous year even in the midst of the crisis.

The microentrepreneur, though, he pays more than 6 percent. The microfinance institutions earn a higher margin to cover salaries for their staff and other operational expenses, including possibly a reasonable profit. Without microfinance, the option for many of those people at the bottom of the pyramid was to stay in misery or go to the loan shark. That's the cruel, brutal choice they had. Then in 1976, in Bangladesh, there was a renaissance of the idea of microfinance. It's actually a very old idea, but it came back in Bangladesh with Professor Muhammad Yunus. Professor Yunus found out that you cannot give money for free, because then it would be in the camp of charity and aid; but you also cannot go up to the level of those loan sharks, those people who profit in a massive way from others' poverty. So it depends very much on the region and even the nation, but everywhere we have to ask, what is the right amount to charge in interest?

Dalai Lama: Wonderful. Very good, very good.

Matthieu Ricard: Muhammad Yunus speaks of what he calls a *selfless economy*. In a selfless economy there will be some profit, but the profit is not meant to accumulate profit for its own sake and for a very limited number of people. Instead it is meant to support social progress, like helping women to get jobs and send their kids to school. At the end of the year, the balance sheet is not how many millions in profit you made, or the bonus you got, but how many people have benefitted from your activities. That's the real balance sheet. You can calculate how efficient you have been by how many kids went to school and how many people were lifted out of poverty. At the 2010 World Economic Forum Annual Meeting in Davos, Yunus proposed that there could be a Wall Street for pro-social businesses that would not be in competition with the regular economic system. It would simply be organized so that people who really want to invest in companies whose chief goal is pro-social would have a structure within which to do it.

I heard from a distinguished French economist that this kind of investment will never attract the big shots, because they want high financial returns on their investments. Therefore there is a natural limitation to this idea, because of the greedy ones who will say that 5 percent is just not enough. They prefer to take risks to try to earn a lot; they believe social progress is not their job.

How do you see the sustainable growth on a larger scale? Do you think there could be a Wall Street of pro-social businesses?

Arthur Vayloyan: I don't know, to be honest, if there could be a pro-social Wall Street. But as to the first question, we do see big shots in the field. The *very* "big shots"— that's your term—don't invest in this type of fund, because you can go in with one thousand dollars or euros or Swiss francs; you don't need to be a millionaire. The big shots create their own funds. They set aside a part of their fortune and put it into an idea of their own.

Sometimes those people don't want to diversify around the globe. Sometimes they want to go in a specific area, like Africa. There is microfinance in Africa, but it hasn't had the impact there that it has had in other regions, like Latin America or Southeast Asia. So they say, why go global? They try to help and support particular regions where, as I showed you, the decline in extreme poverty has not taken place yet. The population is growing rapidly, and with it extreme poverty—the percentage of people living in poverty remains the same. Right now the best that we can say is that the situation in Africa has leveled off.

Antoinette Hunziker-Ebneter: There is the risk in this business, as well as in any other business, of growing too fast. Not because of big investors, but because of big banks. Not Credit Suisse—you have worked in this area in a very professional way for many years—but other big banks are coming into this business, wanting to lend large amounts of money. Sustainable microfinance funding has been successful by lending small amounts. When larger loans are given, it attracts more men and more corruption; and the problem is that men don't pay back the money in the disciplined way that women do. (Women pay back their loans in 98 percent of the cases.[4]) So the microfinance business is getting much riskier than before. This development started last year, because we had the crisis, and as you said, these investments didn't crash in the same way because they are not traded at stock exchanges. So we have to be very careful and check the gender of the lendees and the amount of the loans that microfinance funds are giving.

Matthieu Ricard: There's something else to worry about as well. Of course the number of people who live in extreme poverty has decreased throughout the world, but inequality—the gap between the rich and the poor—has increased twentyfold since the beginning of the twentieth century, and it's still growing very quickly. Right now, according to economist and Nobel laureate Joseph Stiglitz, the ten richest people in the United States own as much as the 98 million poorest people combined. Someone calculated that if it continues at this rate, in 2050 two thousand Americans might own 90 percent of the money. Of course that may not happen, but the trend is for inequality to increase, so how does that affect this funding idea?

Arthur Vayloyan: I think maybe the answer is that money is almost like a magnet. If you have a little money, it's easier to get more money. If you have no money, it's very difficult to get that little money. Adam Smith said that, actually. And once you have a lot of money, it accumulates at a staggering speed, and others can't catch up, which creates this widening inequality gap. We use a definition, a very cruel and somehow simplistic definition, of so-called "extreme poverty." It's a World Bank definition that everyone relies on, from Jeffrey Sachs to us, and that is living on less than $1.25 per day in purchasing power parity. That is how extreme poverty is described. This statistic doesn't show you the gap between the very rich, who get richer and richer, and the poor, but it shows you that despite all the bad news, there is some change. As we saw, to have "only" 20 percent of the world's population living in extreme poverty represents progress, historically speaking.

Two hundred years ago, it was just the other way. In 1820, the World Bank estimates, 80 percent of the world lived in extreme poverty.[5] If we consider only this measure, it looks like we've done pretty well. But there are so many things that we have to take care of. Every day we have seventeen thousand children dying from hunger. We cannot just say there's been good progress, let's relax. We have to become more active.

13

The Barefoot College

Sanjit "Bunker" Roy

Sanjit "Bunker" Roy is an Indian educator, social entrepreneur, and activist. He is the founder of the Barefoot College, an informal, alternative educational institution based on the idea that traditional and indigenous knowledge should be applied to solving rural problems. His innovative educational model has now spread to fifty-four other countries, mostly in Africa.

Bunker's life changed completely in 1965 after a trip to rural Bihar showed him the immense knowledge possessed by illiterate villagers whom the world called "uneducated." Bunker described the evolution of the Barefoot College as a place to harness that wisdom. He spoke with Gert and His Holiness about rural-urban migration. Matthieu ended the presentation by affirming the potential of low-overheard NGOs like Barefoot.

Your Holiness, in 1956 when I was a very young boy, you came to my school, the Doon School, with the Panchen Lama.[1] I got a very snobbish, elitist, expensive education in India. I went to the Doon School, and I went to St. Stephen's College in Delhi.[2] And my life was all set, because you know what Indian families are like. My family had my future all laid out for me. Jobs were waiting for me. I thought the formal education that I had was good, because it made me arrogant. It made me conceited. It made me think that I had the answers to everything. You know what such expensive education can do to you, Your Holiness? It can destroy you.

Then there was the Bihar famine in 1965, when Jayaprakash Narayan appealed to India's young people to come to the villages to help.[3] I went, and it changed my life. When I came back, I told my mother that I'd like to live and work in a village. My mother almost went into a coma; she couldn't understand what had happened to me after just fourteen days in Bihar. Then she asked, "What do you want to do in a village?" I said, "I want to be an unskilled laborer digging wells for water in Rajasthan." That upset her even more. She didn't speak to me for many years, because she thought I had brought the image of the family down by going and living in a village.

I first went to the village where I've worked for the last forty years in 1971. When I arrived, the elders came to me and said, "Are you running from the police?" I said, "No." "You couldn't get a government job?" I said, "No, that's not true." "Did you fail in your exams? What are you doing here? Is there something wrong with you?"

This was the attitude that the formal system gave you in India, and it's probably true all over the world—that you are supposed to go up, to Paris, Zurich, New York. If you come back to the village, it is a punishment; something is dreadfully wrong with you. But for five years I dug wells as an unskilled laborer, and I was exposed to the most extraordinary skills and knowledge and wisdom that very poor people have. It does not come from books. It does not come from a university. It does not come from colleges. You don't read about it—you have to feel it. I felt that this extraordinary knowledge and skill and wisdom needed to be brought into mainstream thinking. That was when I started the Barefoot College in Rajasthan, in a very small village called Tilonia.

When I spoke to the elders about what I was doing, they said, "Please, there are some things that you must not do in the college." They said, "Don't bring in anyone with a degree or paper qualification." So it is the only college in India, indeed in the world that I know of, where anyone with a PhD or a master's degree is disqualified to teach. It has to be someone who works with his hands. It has to be someone who respects the knowledge and skills that are available in village communities, which in this setting are much more important than information that comes from the West. It has to be someone who believes in simplicity. Barefoot is one of the few colleges in India that believes in the lifestyle and work style of Mahatma Gandhi. We sit on the floor. We eat on the floor. We work on the floor, and no one gets more than $150 a month ever, because you don't come for the money, you come for the challenge. You come to work with the poor, and you have to be able to set an example that other people will match and follow.

I do not accept today's economic model, because it is top-down. It comes from the top somewhere in the West, somewhere in Delhi, and they bring it down to a village. When there is so much knowledge and so many skills below, why aren't we developing that first? If that knowledge is not up to date, or needs to be upgraded, then you bring in outside knowledge. But first you develop the capacity and competence of the very poor to develop themselves. This is the most important message that I think we need to convey to the West.

Using village skills and local, low-cost materials, we constructed the Barefoot College Tilonia campus in 1986 at $1.50 per square foot.

It was built by someone who still can't read and write today. At Barefoot we believe you can apply the most sophisticated technology, but not at the expense of traditional wisdom and local people's technology. We are the only college in India that is fully solar-energized. We have forty-five kilowatts of panels on the roofs of the buildings providing power for forty computers, the telephone switchboard, the Internet, seven hundred lights and fans, the library, the dining hall, an

Figure 13.1: The women in this photo do not know how to read or write, but they have been trained as electronics engineers.

audiovisual room, and a solar-operated dentist's chair. Everything works off the sun. The college also uses solar power for cooking; we only use cooking gas during emergencies. The solar energy system was installed and fabricated by a Hindu priest, who completed only eight years of schooling. He knows more about solar energy than anybody I know, from any university, anywhere in the world.

We said, where is it written that just because you can't read and write, you cannot become an architect? You cannot become a dentist? You cannot become a water or solar engineer? It's only in our minds that we think that you have to know how to read and write to do these things. We starting taking people from the village who had never had a formal education, and we trained them to work with computers and be teachers, doctors, engineers, and architects.

This solar cooker (see figure 13.2A) was fabricated by four women. It's the most sophisticated parabolic solar cooker you can have, Your Holiness. These women are illiterate, but they are incredibly precise. They have formed an association where they fabricate solar cookers and sell them in villages to make sure that people don't have to rely solely on kerosene and wood for cooking. They also supply solar cookers to pre-primary schools. Solar-cooked food is now provided to more than a thousand children between the ages of one and five in our area.

We also believe that traditional culture should not lose its importance and relevance, so we use traditional arts like puppetry to convey vital social messages. In places in India where there is no radio, no written word, and no television, traditional puppetry is still very important. A transfer of technology has taken place from string puppets that can only be watched by fifty people in a closed room to glove

Figure 13.2A: A parabolic solar cooker on the roof of the dining hall at the Barefoot College's Tilonia campus. This solar cooker provides food for sixty staff members twice a day.

puppets that can be seen by five thousand people in schools and marketplaces.

The college believes in the tremendous power of traditional communicators like puppeteers and street players performing in the open. The script is impromptu. The plays are interactive and are often stopped in the middle by someone in the audience who wants to ask questions. Our puppeteers reach over 100,000 people every year, performing the role of doctor, teacher, lawyer, psychoanalyst, and engineer as they go.

We run 225 schools in six states that are attended by 7,000 children, out of which 5,500 are girls. We run the schools at night, because in the morning most children are looking after cattle and

Figure 13.2B: Shehnaz, a thirty-year-old illiterate woman, fabricates a sophisticated clock that turns the solar cooker with the sun.

goats and sheep. All of the schools are solar lit. All of the students participate in an election. We believe that the children must know about citizenship, must know about democracy, must know how to elect the right leader; so we have an election, and every three years we have a children's parliament. Our prime minister is twelve years old: she looks after twenty goats in the morning, but in the evening she is the prime minister. She has a cabinet, and they monitor and supervise their own schools. Every decision that the children make, we have to implement, because it's the cabinet, after all.

In 2001, the Barefoot College and the children's parliament won the World's Children's Prize Honorary Award for our work in bringing education to underserved children, especially girls. The prime minister of our parliament, a girl named Devaki who had never left

Figure 13.3: Supported by Barefoot, performers use glove puppets to convey messages about social issues such as domestic violence and the importance of clean drinking water and education. The puppets are made out of recycled World Bank reports.

her village in her life, went to Sweden and accepted the prize from the queen of Sweden. The queen of Sweden couldn't believe that this young girl, twelve years old, was not dazzled by anything around her. She asked me to ask the prime minister where she got her confidence. Devaki looked very insulted, looked straight at the queen, and said, "Please tell her I'm the prime minister!"

After we solar electrified several villages in Rajasthan, we extended the technology to other parts of the country. We have solar electrified six hundred villages all over India. We went to Ladakh in the Nubra Valley near the Siachen Glacier, where the temperatures reach -40 degrees Fahrenheit. We asked a woman in Ladakh, "What is the benefit you have received from solar energy?" She thought for a minute and said, "This is the first time I can see my husband's face in the winter."

In 2005–2006 we also extended the Barefoot model to Afghanistan. We went there and said, "Why don't we take women to train as engineers?" The men said, "Not possible. They don't even leave their rooms, and you want to take them to India?" I said, "I promise, to make a concession, to take the husbands along too." So the husbands came. In 2005 we educated these women, and then they solar electrified the first five villages ever in Afghanistan. My best woman solar engineer is Gul Bahar, a grandmother who is fifty-five years old. She is illiterate, but she has solar electrified two hundred houses in Afghanistan. I asked her to speak to some engineers in Afghanistan. She taught an engineer the difference between AC and DC. The engineer didn't know.

Today the three Afghan women we trained have trained twenty-seven more women, and they have solar electrified a hundred villages in Afghanistan. When I went to the United Nations, I said, "We brought three women and three men to India, trained them, bought 140 solar panels, transported them, and solar electrified five villages—and we did it all in six months." I asked them, "Guess how much it cost?" The UN people, they're used to things being very expensive, and they couldn't guess how much it could be. I said, "It's the cost of one UN consultant sitting for one year in Kabul." So we said, "This is a scandal that there are seven hundred consultants sitting in Kabul from the UN, and there is not one village that they have solar electrified today."

We have had such amazing success with women, but we have also learned an important lesson, Your Holiness, which is that men are untrainable. Men are restless, they are compulsively mobile, and they all want a certificate. And the moment you give them a certificate—

Dalai Lama: But you yourself?

Bunker Roy: Your Holiness, I'm a lost cause. (*laughter*)

Dalai Lama: Really wonderful. Really wonderful. Yes.

Bunker Roy: The moment you give them a certificate, they will leave the village and look for a job in a city. So for me, the best investment is in grandmothers. The grandmothers are between forty and fifty years old. They are the most mature, they are the most tolerant, and they have so much courage.

Some of the grandmothers we train are from Africa. They are illiterate, they have never been outside their villages, and they come for six months to the Barefoot College. They have to be from a village that they have never left; the government of India has given me a blank check for students like these. Through sign language, and sight and sound—without the written word, without the spoken word—in six months we train them to be solar engineers. They all talk to each other. They cannot understand a word of what they are saying to each other because they speak Jola, Wolof, French, Swahili, but the body language is so good that you can see that they want to learn. The first thing we tell them is, "You are some of the only women in your country to become engineers, so please remember, you are ambassadors." When they go back, they walk out of the plane with so much confidence. It is amazing to see the transformation. So Your Holiness, if you know a grandmother whom you would like to send to the Barefoot College, we'd be delighted.

We have worked with women from thirty countries in Africa. We have trained over three hundred grandmothers from these countries. We have solar electrified seven thousand houses, and it's all at the cost of $2 million, which is what Mr. Jeff Sachs spends on one village in Africa, only one village. So if there's so much money, why don't we spread it around? I will end with a quotation from Mahatma Gandhi, who said, "First they ignore you, then they laugh at you, then they fight you, then you win."

Dalai Lama: Really wonderful. I have a conviction—and I've been telling my Indian friends this—that in India, real transformation must start from the countryside and the villages. That is the nature of your work. Then I think India can be an example for the rest of the world, and particularly the southern hemisphere, the poorer countries. I think that of 6 billion human beings, the majority are poor. So without much expense, real transformation can happen. That's the real hope—that real change for 6 billion human beings can come in the way you're describing. A few big cities in India, like Bangalore or Hyderabad, have rapidly developed, but that's not the real transformation of India. Real transformation must come from villages. So I really appreciate what you are doing. In the meantime, I want some of your semiliterate teachers and engineers to come to our Tibetan settlements in different parts of India. We also see young Tibetans very eager for some certificate; they usually go to the big cities for a job. The village is supposed to be an agriculture settlement, but the more able-bodied people who have some education prefer to leave. Our fundamental plan is becoming difficult. So I really want to invite you to show us your method, when you have some time.

Bunker Roy: Your Holiness, for you, anytime.

Dalai Lama: And then eventually China, too, I think, should learn this. The coastal areas are very developed, but in the interior, they are very, very poor. So there also, I think India should be the guru on development and transformation. Not Karl Marx, but an Indian guru!

Gert Scobel: There are two things you mentioned in passing that I want to talk about. One is migration, which His Holiness just mentioned too—the idea that if you have a degree, you go to the city. Why the attraction to the city? How can you prevent this kind of migration? And talking about China and India, in India you have a very long democratic tradition. In China, you don't have that. What kind of difference do you think that makes?

Bunker Roy: The major difference is that every Indian citizen has a right to speak out against the establishment. India sees a difference between being anti-establishment and anti-government. China has a top-down, rigid political structure that does not encourage dissent or discussion or open debate. India provides the space for individual personal growth; no such space exists in China.

I believe that to prevent migration, you have to develop the quality of life in villages. If you create jobs, if you improve the drinking water situation, if you improve the lighting situation, why should anyone in his right mind go to a slum in Mumbai? Our job is to make sure that we improve the quality of life in villages so people don't migrate because of economic pressure or environmental pressure. The Barefoot College believes that if you improve the basic services and you give people jobs, jobs with dignity and self-respect, then villagers will stay, and I think that is the answer. And we have found that when we solar electrified villages in Africa, the villager was coming back to his village from the city because he saw solar lighting for the first time. So you can reverse migration by bringing in solar lighting in villages. And you have jobs, because the women, the grandmothers, are being paid by the community to look after repair and maintenance. They are engineers. They are not women anymore.

Dalai Lama: I think it's better to say *women engineers*. "Not women anymore," that's not good.

Bunker Roy: Woman-grandmother-engineer.

Dalai Lama: That's good; that's better.

Matthieu Ricard: I think in all the discussions we have had, there is one very powerful force that we may not have fully considered. It's the grassroots NGOs. There are now millions of NGOs all over the world. Your example, Bunker, is magnificent and humbling, but there are so many other endeavors—some on a smaller scale, and some on a bigger scale, like BRAC, which took 60 million women out of poverty in Bangladesh. There are now young people everywhere, even in developed countries—and many more of them than there were twenty years ago—who say, "I want to go to business school not so I can work on Wall Street, but so I can learn how to do effective humanitarian work." Of course humanitarian work needs to be grounded in the field, not just thought about in business schools, but this trend is encouraging.

I also wanted to give you a small example that goes along with your story. I have a friend in Nepal, Uttam Sanjel, who has been doing work for several years through the support of our humanitarian association, Karuna-Shechen. Uttam was dismayed by the number of kids running around in the streets of Kathmandu and other cities, getting into all kinds of trouble from lack of education. The problem is that the parents come to the cities and have to work very hard. They park the kids in a room during the day and feed them at night. Of course the kids are not going to stay. They start roaming the streets. They start stealing. They start sniffing glue and stuff like that. So our friend went around asking for two pieces of bamboo from each family, with which he constructed a very small school. That was twelve years ago. He had absolutely no money in his pocket. Now there are 20,000 children in those bamboo schools. In two and a half months you can build a school for 2,500 kids with $100,000. That's hard to beat. The idea is to reach 150,000 students in Nepal. Our association helped Uttam build nine of those schools.

Another small example is an Indian Catholic nun, Sister Jessie, who started a small program in a village in Bihar. The first year she gives a chicken to a woman, and gives her a bank account booklet with a little seed money with which she will send her children to school. The husband, who often drinks, has no signature on the account; otherwise he'll empty it to buy some locally made alcohol. Now, if she succeeds, if the kids have attended school the second year, Sister

Jessie will give a goat to that mother. And if the kids continue to go to school, and if the mother manages to keep some small capital from selling goat milk without the husband taking everything, the third year she gets a cow; and the fourth year, she gets help building a better house.

Those are just two examples; there are so many more. These NGOs are very dedicated. They don't have 60 percent overhead like some of the multinational so-called NGOs; they have between 3 and 5 percent overhead. In the case of our small Karuna-Shechen organization, we have only done 120 projects over twelve years, but we have maintained 5 percent overhead. If those great big organizations could fund a hundred NGOs like ours, there would be 10,000 grassroots projects with 5 percent overhead. That would be another way to expand, replicating a good formula many times over rather than making one single huge organization.

NGOs are a very, very powerful force of movement toward a more cooperative, altruistic, dedicated society. Of course, microcredit is encouraging them, but we should also think more about how we can help big, established organizations to become better organized and collaborate more efficiently with small grassroots NGOs so they can make a bigger difference on the ground.

14

Compassionate Leadership

William George

William George is a professor of management practice at Harvard Business School, where he teaches leadership development and ethics. He is the former chairman and CEO of Medtronic. Under his leadership, the company's market capitalization grew from $1.1 billion to $60 billion, averaging a 35 percent increase each year.

Bill discussed the qualities of true leaders—how they are discovered and fostered, what we expect of them, and whose interests they serve. In the business world, as elsewhere, he said it is by serving others first that leaders can find their own happiness. His Holiness ended the presentation by speaking about the need to shift our focus back toward immaterial values and the creation of long-term contentment.

Your Holiness, it's a privilege to be with you. Having heard about all the research everyone here is doing in compassion and altruism, and seen some marvelous applications, I'm very encouraged. I think the question now is, how do we take this on a broad scale to create altruistic organizations that can really transform society and transform economic systems? This is the field I've been studying since I left the corporate world eight years ago, and I am convinced that the key to this is compassionate, authentic leadership. We need a new generation of leaders to step forward and provide this new kind of leadership.

Many people have considered the 2008 economic crisis—we call it the financial meltdown—a failure of economics. I look at it at a deeper level. It's not an economic failure—it is a spiritual failure. Many, many people believed that, in essence, they could find happiness through material wealth, and that the more material wealth they accumulated, the happier they would be. But then they found that just the opposite was the case: they were not happy, and they also did great harm to others.

We have an enormous jobs crisis in the world, where people don't have work. I come from a world where work is good and meaningful, so the lack of jobs has created great destruction. We need to get back to the fact that true meaning can only come from serving other people through compassion, through an altruistic approach that benefits all of society. So that's what I'd like to talk about today.

My basic premise is that compassionate, authentic leadership is essential. It's not just that it's good to have—it's necessary for a healthy society. I'm persuaded by Ernst and others that we need a set of principles by which to operate. We need a set of sanctions for improper behavior, and, more importantly, we need leaders who have a positive impact on individuals, and on organizations, and on society. Without this, I don't think we can achieve a healthy society, because smart people will always find ways around rules.

It's important to think about what's caused the economic failure. I'm disappointed in my generation of leaders; I believe they have failed in their responsibility. That's why I'm working with the next generation. As a result of the failures of leadership in the last decade, there's been a loss of confidence in our leaders, and a loss of trust. If we don't trust our leaders, we have a very serious situation. At Harvard, the Kennedy School has done a study and found that two out of every three people do not trust their leaders. They don't trust their values. They don't trust their ethics. (When I say "ethics," I'm referring to secular ethics here, not any form of religious ethics.)

I think the root cause of the problem is leaders who have placed their self-interest ahead of their responsibility to organizations and to the public. Each of us who takes a leadership role has a deep responsibility to the people we serve. If we put ourselves ahead of them, we have failed in our responsibilities, and we can cause great harm.

I also see a prevalence of extrinsic motivation, of people seeking the acclaim of the external world. In other words, instead of finding inner peace, they're looking for adulation. They're looking for money as a reward. They're looking for power, for fame, for recognition and glory, instead of the intrinsic satisfaction of helping other people, of engaging in a deeper relationship with people and creating good for the world and good for society.

We need a new generation of authentic leaders to step forward, who are genuine and compassionate people. They recognize that the purpose of leading is to serve others and society. Each day, they practice their values. They don't just state them; they actually practice them in their lives. They lead not just with their intellects, but with the whole person in a holistic form of leadership. When I say that, I'm not trying to diminish the role of the intellect. I'm saying that we also have to lead with our hearts, because that's how we build connected relationships. To do this every day requires self-discipline in one's life.

In order for this new generation of leaders to emerge, we need to move away from top-down leadership. For many years we have looked to the person on top as all powerful and we have studied that person, rather than looking for people throughout organizations who have the potential to step up and lead at various levels.

I also believe at a deeper level that people's desires have changed. They have learned the hard way that money is not the goal. There is a deep underlying search for meaning in people's lives. At my former company Medtronic, which makes medical products, our mission and our meaning was to restore people to full life and health. The way we measured ourselves was not by earnings per share but by how many people we helped. My greatest source of pride is that in the time I was there, we went from 300,000 people per year to 10 million people per year who were being restored to fuller, more active lives through our work. We always tried to convey this meaning to people in the company, because that's what inspired them, not the stock price, not the earnings.

The role of the leader in this century is different than in centuries past. It's to bring people together around this sense of meaning, purpose, and values. It is a very difficult task, particularly in organizations that span the globe, to gain that kind of alignment where people believe in the purpose of the organization and practice its values.

The second role of the leader is not to exert power over other people. Many scholars have written about leadership as power. This idea of power suggests a zero-sum game: if I give you power, I have less. But I reject this idea. I think leadership is about empowering other people to lead. What we're trying to do through empowerment is more like love. It can be infinite. If we can empower other people to step up and lead, then we have much stronger organizations, and we can all contribute to the best of our abilities.

Let me give you an example of a woman whom I met at Medtronic many years ago. She was making heart valves. If a human heart valve failed, they could actually take a valve from a pig and use it to replace the failed human heart valve. This woman was the top worker in the plant. When I asked her about her work, she looked at me with passion in her eyes and said, "My job is to make heart valves that save people's lives. I make one thousand heart valves a year. If one valve is defective, someone will die, and I could never live with the idea that I caused the death of another person." But she also said, "You know, when I go home at night, what I'm thinking about is that there are five thousand people in the world today who are alive and healthy because of the products I made."

This woman is an empowered leader. She doesn't have a formal leadership role, and she isn't a supervisor, but everyone looks to her for inspiration. This is the kind of empowered leadership we need to spread much more broadly.

Many people assert that we're there to serve the investor, the owner, the shareholder. To a certain extent that's true, but perhaps more than that, leaders are there to serve their employees and their customers. We are servant leaders, and if we do that job well, then everyone else can do their job well. If we think others are there to serve us, we will fail.

Another important consideration is competition inside organizations. The new mode is collaboration. You heard from Arthur

Vayloyan about microfinance. Microfinance can only take place with the collaboration of people in the village who come together. They form a trust bank. They help each other. How else can it work? Bunker Roy described the implementation of solar power in villages. It's not just the engineer; it's everyone coming together to collaborate, from the person who makes the technology all the way to the workers who install it. At Medtronic we asked our patients to collaborate with us. We need this kind of broad vision of collaboration. This is the new form of leadership we are moving toward.

We've done first-person research by talking in depth with 125 leaders. What in their lives gave them the passion to lead? How did they get through the difficult times in their lives? What we found is that their leadership came not from unique traits or characteristics but from who they were, their inner calling, and their life story. We also learned that leaders are neither born nor made; they are developed. We have to develop our leadership through a series of practices.

Dan Goleman opened up the notion of emotional intelligence, or EQ. We don't spend enough time in school developing this, but it is at the heart of the questions we are all asking ourselves: How do I gain awareness of who I am on the planet? How do I understand my story, and recognize and resolve the sources of my anger, fear, or insecurity? How do I develop genuine humility? Finally, how do I discern the purpose of my leadership? How can I lead? How can I help enhance society?

I have been a meditator for thirty-four years, and I advocate meditation to people as the most important element of my own leadership development. Why? I have found that through the process of meditation, I can gain clarity about complex issues. It triggers creative thought. But most importantly, it helps me develop compassion for myself and others. We all lead very stressful lives. Meditation has been crucial for me to build the resilience to cope with the stresses in my life.

The ultimate role of compassionate leaders is to create organizations that are altruistic, that serve society. What I have found is that this is the only way you can sustain the organization. It's the only way you can sustain your contributions, and the only way you can sustain your leadership. The key is, can the organization create value for everyone it serves—for its customers, its employees, its investors? Does it create that kind of lasting value? This is the essential requirement to create superior performance for the long term. You can make a lot of money in the short term by not doing this, but this is the only way to sustain successful performance in the long term.

To conclude, I think we need a new generation of compassionate, authentic leaders who can positively impact the thousands of people they interact with every day. We need to engage in the development of more leaders who can do this. Not just leaders on top, but leaders throughout organizations, so that many, many people can become those compassionate leaders whose everyday lives are transforming society and bringing altruism to organizations and to economic systems.

Your Holiness, we seek your counsel on that. How can we develop more people who can go out into the world and transform organizations, who are compassionate leaders with a strong inner sense of themselves?

Dalai Lama: Actually, you pointed out one of the key facts: that leaders are not born or made, but cultivated and developed. Another way to develop leaders, I think, is through the training of inner values.

I think many leaders have heard about these things, but they are not fully convinced. So they may say, "Oh, very nice," but they believe it's not fully relevant. The Buddhist concept—this is a concept of Buddhist philosophy, but it can essentially be universal in a secular way—is that everything is interdependent, interconnected. So the development of proper leaders is also related to education and circumstances.

Some people may not agree with what I'm about to say, but before my first visit to Jerusalem, some media people from Israel came to see me, and we talked about the Holocaust. I am a Buddhist, and from my Buddhist viewpoint, I believe that even in Hitler, there was a seed of compassion. He was not necessarily evil at the beginning of his childhood, but due to many circumstances he eventually became so. When I reached Tel Aviv, I was told there were news reports stating, "The Dalai Lama thinks even Hitler is a positive person." What I was saying was that everybody at the time of birth is the same. The potential for good and bad is always there, in everyone.

We must nurture the positive things. Positive emotions are really a benefit to oneself and others. Warmheartedness and a sense of responsibility clearly have an important role in modern society, in every field. And neuroscientists have made very clear the possibility of change in that direction. Training can make a difference, so now it's up to people. I think one important thing we need is some kind of proper plan in education and other fields.

I think that in society as a whole—and this was also true in ancient times—everybody knows that love and compassion are important. All major religious traditions talk about the importance of these things, because society considers them precious. It has been that way for thousands of years. Then eventually science emerged, and technology was invented. Through prayer, good things don't necessarily come immediately. Buddhists today might think, for example, about praying for the next life or the next eon, "That's too far off." Technology, on the other hand, brings immediate results, so naturally people are very excited about that. I think that has started a trend toward forgetting our inner values. Material and matter have nothing to do with compassion. But for the last few centuries, we have been very excited about them and have experienced their immense usefulness.

Now the time has come in which we are experiencing the limitations of material values. And we are facing many unnecessary problems. So gradually we are returning to our basic human values with a new appreciation. We are still human beings. We have the experience of pleasure and pain. Material values and technology cannot change these things, and they cannot bring inner peace. The shift began in the late twentieth century, with new experiences, new interests, and new awareness. Now, at the beginning of this twenty-first century, respected thinkers are pointing us to essential ingredients that are lacking in our society. I think this is a wonderful, hopeful trend. Even though the fruits of our efforts may not materialize fully within our lifetime, we are starting something; coming generations will follow. Within this century maybe there will be a better, more compassionate human society. Then compassionate leadership will also come.

Conclusion

Compassion Is Not a Luxury

Joan Halifax with His Holiness the Dalai Lama and Richard Davidson, John Dunne, and Ernst Fehr

Roshi Joan Halifax, PhD, is a Buddhist teacher, Zen priest, anthropologist, and author. She is founder, co-abbot, and head teacher at the Upaya Zen Center, a Buddhist monastery in Santa Fe, New Mexico. Her work focuses on engaged and applied Buddhism, particularly the contemplative care of the dying.

Joan moderated the final session of the conference, joining Richie, John, and Ernst in conversation with His Holiness to recap the previous days' discussion and address questions that arose during the events, including the role of gender and intelligence in altruism. His Holiness reminded us of the ultimate importance of fostering secular ethics, and closed out the proceedings by acknowledging the many hopeful signs of progress.

Joan Halifax: Your Holiness, this is our final session, and on behalf of Mind and Life, I want to thank you for dedicating so much time to this exploration. It is a true pioneering effort on the part of Mind and Life. We were curious as to how this would unfold. This is not the first time that economics and neuroscience have been brought together, but this dialogue is still quite new. Bringing applied economics into the discussion by hearing from people like Antoinette and Bunker is wonderful, because we get to look at the very principles that you address in your teachings being applied in the world today by people who are not Buddhists, but who have altruism as a kind of North Star in their lives, as well as a very deep concern about the well-being of people and the environment.

I remember many years ago you said the following words, which have been a kind of North Star for me personally. You said, "Compassion is not a luxury. It is a necessity in order for the human being to survive." I think that idea is a driving force behind what we are doing here today.

I want to bring another quote into the circle of our exploration. This is from a past president of the United States, Franklin Delano Roosevelt. Roosevelt said, "We have always known that heedless self-interest was bad morals. Now we know that it is bad economics."

So we have been sitting together with the following question: Can we envision an economic system that delivers both material prosperity and human and environmental well-being? If we bring it down to the simplest, most direct question, do such economic systems currently exist, and can we foster or develop them? Underneath that question is another question that has been explored by Tania and Richie and others. The question is, what roles do altruism, empathy, and compassion play in modern economic development?

Thanks to Richie, Tania, Dan, and Joan, we've looked inside the human and the animal brain to explore the neurological basis of altruism, empathy, and compassion. We've explored economic research on altruism and generosity, thanks to Ernst, Richard, and Bill Harbaugh. We've heard about inspiring endeavors in global and local economic systems, thanks to Antoinette, Arthur, Bunker, and Bill George. We've also heard a Buddhist perspective on altruism and compassion, thanks to John and Matthieu.

Ernst really brought into focus the value of democracy in the world today and how this affects the domain of public goods, which are not just material. They are also the domain of what we've been exploring—altruism. We've looked at the place of strong civic norms in their effect on economic systems; Ernst brought up the example of the situation in Greece, and talked about altruistic sanctions in a very interesting way. But how can we have altruistic economic systems that don't require sanctions? I think that's a question that many of us are sitting with.

Very importantly, both Tania and Richie talked about the fact that we can actually train the human mind to have greater altruism, greater compassion, greater empathy, and more resilience in a world that is quite complex. We've had the opportunity to look at some of the research in social psychology and in neuroscience with regard to empathy, empathic concern, empathic distress, altruism, and compassion. These are fundamental mental qualities making a difference in the world today, in the direction of good, and I think that's why we were so enthusiastic listening to Bunker and Antoinette and Arthur. We suddenly thought, "Ah, we could have an economic system that is based on healthy altruism. We could have a compassion-based economic system."

Westerners are very much oriented toward evidence, so I want to thank you, Richie, for the pioneering work you've done in exploring contemplative practice and how the brain works, the neural substrates of compassion, and so forth. It would be wonderful if you could summarize some of what we've covered, and then enter into a dialogue with His Holiness.

Richie Davidson: Thank you, Joan, and thank you, Your Holiness. Before I begin a little bit of summary, I'd like to reflect that this is the twentieth meeting of the Mind and Life Institute's scientific dialogues with Your Holiness. Over the course of this long time together, we've had many different branches of science come together, but this is our very first meeting that has brought economics into our formal discussion. I wanted to simply pause and express to you, Your Holiness, the incomparable gratitude that I think all of us feel for the inspiration that you have provided. There is no other world leader who has spent so much time with scientists and scholars, and we are so grateful.

Dalai Lama: Actually, I am not like those leaders who have a country, who have a lot of work. I'm quite free. So it's partly to pass the time! (*laughter*)

Joan Halifax: That's real humility!

Richie Davidson: What I'd like to do is to summarize some of the key themes that have come out of this meeting, and through this summary ask Your Holiness some specific questions that have come up over the course of our dialogue together. We began in the first session with a discussion of empathy and altruism and their psychological and neuroscientific bases. We talked about the empathy-altruism hypothesis, which claims that pro-social motivation—the motivation to help others, which is associated with a feeling of empathy—is directed toward the ultimate aim of benefiting another person, rather than more egotistic goals. The evidence that we heard supports the empathy-altruism hypothesis: the motivation that arises from feelings of empathy is an altruistic, rather than an egotistic, motivation.

We also learned about some neuroscientific bases of empathy. When people are exposed to the pain of others, they show changes in their brain that are similar to some of the changes that the person who is actually in pain displays. One of the areas of the brain that we discussed is the insula, or the interoceptive area. This is an area of the brain that has important relationships with the body. We also learned about the concept of schadenfreude, which is the idea that a person can actually experience joy at seeing another's suffering. The specific experiment where this was demonstrated was when a participant viewed an unjust person experiencing pain. Men (though not women) showed changes in reward areas of the brain when they saw the unfair person receiving pain; these changes were associated with the desire for revenge.

Now, Your Holiness, this was one of several instances over the course of this meeting where differences between men and women were reported. Bunker told us that men were not educable, and he described very beautifully the solar engineer grandmothers. So I'd like to ask you, Your Holiness, is there anything that we can glean from the Buddhist tradition about gender differences? This has come up both in practical areas in our work as well as in basic research, and we would be very interested to know if there's anything you can share.

Dalai Lama: I think all neurons, and different mental states—the gross and subtle levels of mind and energy—are 100 percent the same in both. Men and women are basically the same, except for some differences in organs. In the case of Buddhism, the Buddha essentially gave equal rights to both genders. At that time in India there was some discrimination, but Buddha gave equal opportunities to males and females for full ordination within his order. Of course, in the Vinaya texts,[1] because males were considered higher in the society at that time, one does see some elements of discriminations reflected in the hierarchy of the monastic order.

Thupten Jinpa: Generally in the Buddhist tradition, and Buddhist thought as a whole, there is an association of the male in the general sense—the masculine—with compassion, and the feminine with wisdom.

Dalai Lama: I think it's important that one's mother is the example, among people and even among animals, of the most cherished being. The mother is the source of maximum affection you receive. In the Tibetan language we speak of "all mother sentient beings"—*ma gyur sem chen tamché.*[2] This is very powerful and has a special kind of resonance. But if you try to reverse it and say "all father sentient beings," it doesn't sound right. There is, I think, something different about females. Of course, as a result of our multidisciplinary meetings like this, I understand that biologically, the female has more sensitivity to others' pain.

I think many of you already know this, so I'll be brief. In very ancient times, perhaps some hundred thousand years ago, the concept of leadership did not exist among humans. There were very small communities in which everybody—father, mother, everybody—worked together, and whatever they had, they shared. Then eventually populations increased, life became a little more sophisticated comparatively, and troublemakers emerged. So in order to bring more stability to the community, the concept of leadership was developed.

At that time there was no education to be the basis for dominance; it was only physical power, as it was among other animals. I think among elephants, the mothers are the dominant leaders. Maybe female elephants are a little stronger than males, I don't know. Among humans, in any case, male dominance emerged. If I may say so, perhaps some religious concepts also helped influence that way of thinking.

Now, the idea of *ahimsa*, nonviolence based on compassion, and the concept of religious harmony, these two things are of Indian heritage. Therefore I consider myself a proud messenger of India. These days I also describe myself as a son of India. My understanding and way of thinking related to these values comes from the Indian Nalanda tradition.[3] And physically, for the last fifty-one years, my body has survived on India's dal, rice, and chapati, so I am truly a son of India.

I usually feel really proud to say I'm a son of India, but a few days ago, at a gathering of religious leaders, I also said: "We carry these thousand-year-old Indian traditions, but within our own country the caste system and discriminations still exist. The constitution provides equality, but some bad societal habits from centuries ago persist. We must look at these things. Even though some of these things may be part of India's traditional culture, the time has come for us to change these things that are obstructive." Anyway, this is just an aside.

To get back to what I was saying earlier, gradually, over the course of human history, education has taken a more important role. It brought greater equality between the male and the female. But male dominance still exists. Most leaders, I think, are male. Now the time has come when ability or vision or intelligence or education alone is not sufficient; we need a compassionate heart to be seen as a quality of leadership. So now we are talking about the importance of altruism, of compassion. The time has come for the development of warm hearts, not just smart brains. Here females should take a more active leadership role in promoting the value of compassion.

That is my view. Eventually, I think, the majority of leaders will be women—the more compassionate women. Some women are not compassionate!

Joan Halifax: We won't name names!

Dalai Lama: But generally women are more compassionate, so if we have a majority of women leaders, the troubles we face may be reduced. Sometimes I think—whether it's true or not, I don't know—that many problems can easily be solved if you approach them in a spirit of dialogue and a respect for others' interests. But the prejudiced "I"—"I'll never lose or accept failure"—gets in the way. The other side also takes that position. Then how can you solve problems? We males—with our excessive "I, I, we!"—create obstacles to solving many problems. So the time has come; we men may resign now.

In the Buddhist way of thinking—of course, I am Buddhist, so I am biased in this way—the main idea is the equality of all sentient beings, with no distinction based on sex or even different forms of life, whether animals or insects. I sincerely practice these Buddhist concepts, but still, my relationship with the mosquito is sometimes not very good.

Richie Davidson: Well, that's a good segue to the issue of the relationship between empathy and compassion, which was also discussed in our sessions. The way empathy has been conceptualized by Western scientists in many cases has to do with the experience of the pain of another; or, in a more Buddhist framework, with the experience of the unbearable nature of suffering. In some of the preliminary work that Tania has done with Matthieu using fMRI scans, we saw that the transition from empathy to compassion was one that was accompanied by a tremendous change in Matthieu's experience. And this provided some insight into what it is when people describe "burnout"; it may be the experience of empathy in the absence of compassion.

Other research shows that there are other differences, sometimes quite large ones, in the brain when novice practitioners begin compassion training, compared to longer-term practitioners. So this leads to a question for Your Holiness. I wonder if you can describe for us the evolution, the changes that occur, as a person begins to train to cultivate compassion. What are the stages that may occur early in the practice, compared with later in the practice, and how does the experience of compassion transform over time?

Dalai Lama: Positive emotions like empathy have their limitations. We need the help of intelligence; intelligence brings purpose and goals. Generally speaking, when you see the possibility of overcoming suffering, your concern for that suffering becomes much stronger and more realistic. Without that possibility, what you have is a feeling of concern, some wishful thinking, a lack of enthusiasm, a sense of difficulty. As a result you may feel helpless, discouraged, or demoralized. So the combination of wisdom and compassionate methods is essential. These must go side by side. You can use your cognitive abilities to try to understand the situation and see if there is a way out, a means of overcoming it. The more you understand the situation, the greater your enthusiasm for doing something about it.

I think recognition of the value of empathy or compassion is a function of wisdom and awareness. Animals have a very limited biological capacity to feel concern for their companions; I don't think intelligence is involved. But we human beings—the other day we touched on biased versus unbiased compassion, or compassion not based on attachment. Only human beings can develop that unbiased form of compassion, because it requires intelligence.

Why do we need compassion? Our wisdom or intelligence tells us that it brings inner strength, inner peace. It also brings benefits to others; and we face many unnecessary problems due to the lack of it. All of this is the work of intelligence, and in order to develop that kind of intelligence, we have to develop a holistic way of seeing the bigger picture.

Consider a plant. It has no feeling, no experience of pain and pleasure. Recently, some scientists have said that if you take two of the same type of plant, and you scold one and praise the other, the praised plant grows better. Some scientists said something like that, didn't they?

Richie Davidson: Not scientists!

Dalai Lama: Not scientists? Oh, then, very good. I need that kind of answer. In classical Indian philosophical traditions there were debates on this question of the life of plants. The Buddhists say a plant has no feeling, no experience of suffering and pleasure, while the Jains hold the opposite view.

Firstly we have to have knowledge of pain, and make that distinction between pain and pleasure. Then we—not only we humans, but also animals that experience pain and pleasure—know pain, and know that nobody wants it. Then according to the Buddhist concept of the law of causality, we investigate. Where does the pain come from? What are the main causes and conditions? With a certain mental attitude, even physical pain can bring deeper satisfaction. It is all the work of intelligence and holistic knowing. Through intelligence, you can find some purpose, some usefulness, for physical pain, and then mentally welcome it.

Two years ago when I went through surgery, I felt a little anxiety, but my intelligence was telling me the surgery was necessary. There was also an immense effect from the faces of the specialists, showing big smiles and genuine affection. I felt safe.

Holistic vision, the wider perspective, is very important. It brings conviction and peace of mind. A more calm, compassionate mind brings inner strength and self-confidence. It reduces stress, tension, anxiety, fear. If you don't see holistically but just feel your immediate feelings, compassion can seem silly. It's better to remain indifferent, objective, acting like we are part of a machine with no feeling. That's the scientific way—completely objective, no feeling.

Richie Davidson: Thank you, Your Holiness.

Joan Halifax: Thank you, Richie. Ernst, thank you for your patience. I also want to express a lot of gratitude to you. I think your collaboration with Tania, and what you're doing at the University of Zurich, is really extraordinary. It's groundbreaking in the field of economics; you're on a leading edge. So we'd appreciate your reflections on what you see for the future.

Ernst Fehr: The topic of this session is reflection, integration, and future directions for research and policy. I want to split my short presentation into two parts. One is the take-home messages from this dialogue. What did we learn over these two and a half days? We still have huge challenges before us, so I'd also like to talk about them. And then I have some questions for Your Holiness. Maybe you can help us in solving these challenges.

We have seen in Joan Silk's talk that there are some strong differences between humans and animals. In nonhuman animals, altruistic behavior is frequent, but it is largely confined to close kin or group members. Even in regards to our closest relatives, the chimpanzees, there is some very serious evidence that challenges the view that they have concern for others.

That is very different from the human case. Human altruism goes far beyond what we see in the animal kingdom, because it is not limited to kin or group members. Science has shown that humans do have concern for the welfare of others; we can extend our altruism even to anonymous strangers.

However, this altruistic behavior in humans often takes a conditional form by depending on our observing the altruism of others, and that's a mixed blessing. It's a reason for hope, because our altruistic behavior provides a good example and induces others to do as we do. But because of the existence of individuals who behave selfishly, we also have bad examples. In this competition between good and bad examples, we have to find a way to foster the good examples.

We have seen over the last two days that altruism is imprinted in the human brain. It's not just at the behavioral level that we see it. The very same reward areas in the brain that are activated when I get material resources are also activated when I behave altruistically and provide benefits to others. That's a further reason for hope. We have the chance to change our biology in favorable ways. There is even some evidence that hints that behaving altruistically may make us happier.

These facts are increasingly recognized in the behavioral and social sciences. When I started researching these questions twenty years ago, I got dismissive and patronizing smiles from my colleagues, but today it's much more widely accepted. It's really penetrating science, and one could say there is even a little revolution happening, at least in economics, turning it from a dismal science into a noble science.

We have also seen that if we don't take into account the fact that humans have the capacity for altruism in their motivational and behavioral repertoire, we really don't understand how our society works. We don't understand how markets work. We don't understand organizations, politics, family life. We are unable to understand even our own evolution if we neglect the fact that a substantial share of humans have a propensity for altruism. If we want to improve our world, we have to take our altruistic nature into account.

As this broader perspective is being taken by an increasing number of scientists, there has also been an increase in happiness research. There is now a large body of research that tells us what is important for our happiness. It's no longer speculation. We know that in developed economies—and in developing economies, but particularly in developed economies—a major source of happiness comes from good relations with our spouse, with our friends, and with our colleagues. Maintaining good social relations is key, and our current economic system does not put enough value on this. That's very important. We have to work in that direction, change the incentives, perhaps even change our personalities if possible, to put more emphasis on that.

There are also various obstacles that we have to take into account. One major obstacle to human happiness is envy. That was shown in Richard Layard's talk, and other happiness research also clearly points in that direction. It's interesting and also somewhat uncomfortable to acknowledge this fact, but it is a fact that people suffer if others to whom they compare themselves earn more. This is a very destructive emotion that raises the important question of how we can overcome it.

This brings me to the challenges. We've learned a lot, and we know the obstacles. Now what are the challenges? Here I want to say something very personal. We humans have the capacity sometimes to convince ourselves about something that we believe very strongly, without really knowing whether it is true. I am no exception. I have had my prejudices in my scientific career, and I had to learn that some of what I believed was wrong. So it's very important that we remain open and that we clearly distinguish between what we really know and what we only believe that we know. In that spirit, let me formulate these challenges.

One of the unanswered questions in my view is, are there persistent personality traits in the degree of altruism across time and situations, and if so, how can they be explained? Which factors shape an altruistic personality? This leads to the immediate question of how we can change people's personalities. In the same vein, can altruism be nurtured by the right education? I believe it can. I believe it can, but I don't know it can. You see, I want to believe it; I want it to be true. But if I'm honest, I must say I don't know. Can we avoid envy, or is it a part of human nature? If we can avoid it, how? What is the time scale over which change can occur? We know that if we put a small child into a room and leave her alone for twelve years, only feeding her—there have been such cruel cases—and denying her any social interaction, the child doesn't learn to speak a language. If a child has been deprived of social interactions with other human beings for a sufficiently long time, the child seems incapable of learning to speak a language afterward. So there are critical time windows. Is there a critical time window for the nurturing of altruism? Let us be honest: we don't know.

Maybe the biggest of all questions, at least for this conference and for His Holiness is, do we need Buddhism to nurture an altruistic society? I am not a Buddhist; that's why I want to know. What are the elements in Buddhism that are critical, that can be transferred to the West, that help us to take the best of Buddhism? What components are crucial to achieve what we want to achieve—that is, more altruistic people and a better society?

Joan Halifax: Your Holiness, Ernst's last question is a really important one, and I would ask if you would for just a few minutes talk about what you feel in Buddhism can be translated into the non-Buddhist world as useful to engender a civil society.

Dalai Lama: For more than two thousand years, different religions have coexisted on this planet. I think India is a particularly good example. There, all the major world traditions exist. People are diverse and of many dispositions. We need different religions; that's clear.

Jainism and Buddhism have no concept of a creator, but believe in the law of causality, which I think is quite close to Darwinian theories of evolution. All the major religious traditions—Christianity, Islam, Hinduism, and Judaism—have a certain concept of God as a creator. These traditions place the creator at the center and have a very strong faith in the creator, and that reduces the extreme, self-centered feeling of "I" and ego. You've completely submitted to God. After you've submitted yourself totally to God, and recognized that all creatures are created by God, there is naturally a reason to develop respect and love. One of my Muslim friends said, "The genuine Muslim, the genuine practitioner of Islam, must love all creatures, because all creatures are created by Allah." That is their way, and it is sufficient. The Buddhist theory of selflessness is a different approach, but has a similar effect.

But the problem is that even knowing these things, one may not take them seriously. Another problem is that there are many nonbelievers, who may in fact constitute a large portion of the population. I think many scientists belong in that category. Some scientists, of course, are very religiously minded. One scientist who is almost my guru—Carl von Weizsäcker, the great physicist—was very religiously minded.

The problem is that the entirety of humanity needs altruism or empathy, not necessarily as part of their religious faith but to reduce certain problems we are facing today due to their absence. We have to tackle the root causes. That's our task now. The time has come for that. This is not about this group of people or that group of people, but about 7 billion human beings. If we try to promote these

things on the basis of religion, it will not be universal. That reality
brings us to the conclusion that we must find a way to promote those
values within a secular and inclusive perspective. All major religious
traditions have a similar grounding in them.

Regarding Buddhism, I mentioned earlier the Nalanda tradition,
the Sanskrit Buddhist tradition. This can be divided into three parts:
the aspects of science, Buddhist philosophy or concepts, and Buddhist
religion. Let's leave Buddhist religion aside. The scientific elements
of Buddhist thought have a very detailed explanation of mind and emotion. Regarding Buddhist concepts, I mentioned the concept of interde-
pendency. There's no creator, no absolute one thing, but everything
arises from causes and conditions, so everything is related. That is
the Buddhist concept that implies the necessity of compassion, of a
compassionate society, a compassionate humanity. This doesn't have
to be associated with the Buddhist religion. You can remain a Christian or a nonbeliever, or even be anti-religious. If you really feel all
religion is bad, okay: be a kinder person, because your happiness is
related to the happiness of others. You have to take care of others'
well-being because of your own interest.

I think Buddhist scientific explanations provide a fuller knowledge of emotion, and scientists have helped tremendously to show
that, with training, emotional habits can change. These are very
good results. There are clear indications that the use of imagination
and visualization can actually change our way of thinking and our perception. It's a fact, not mere illusion, and not blind faith. But it
should not require a Buddhist religious practice, just aspects of Buddhist science, which can provide more information about how to
tackle the mind and about the Buddhist concept that everything is
interrelated.

For those people who strongly believe that God is central and absolute, that concept may be problematic. One of my Christian friends, a very good monk, Brother Wayne, does wonderful work. One day he was showing interest in the Buddhist concept of emptiness or independency. I told him, because we know each other very well, "This is not your business." I said that because I fear if a believer analyzes this matter deeply, it may affect his or her total submission to God, or belief in God. I do not want that.

There are so many different religious traditions, but in some cases, monotheistic religious people place too much emphasis on God, God, God. We respect all religions. We really admire how much these traditions have contributed through thousands of years to millions of people. That is sufficient reason to respect, admire, and appreciate them. But from a critical philosophical viewpoint of Buddhist thought, rigorous critiques have been made against the concept of a creator. As someone who has been trained in classical Buddhist thought—I sometimes describe myself as a staunch Buddhist—I am thoroughly familiar with these logical arguments critiquing theism. This, however, does not and should not deter a Buddhist from maintaining a deep respect, even reverence, for the great theistic spiritual traditions.

Now, do we need Buddhism for nurturing an altruistic society? No, but you can take some techniques and some knowledge from Buddhism. That's my view.

Richie Davidson: About fifty years ago most people in Western cultures didn't regularly practice physical exercise, and then scientific research began to show that the regular practice of physical exercise is good for one's health. What we see today is that many people have incorporated regular physical exercise into their weekly routine, and people who do this know that it's not something they can just practice for a few months and then enjoy the benefit for the remainder of their life. They must continue practicing.

The scientific research is beginning to show that mental exercise, mental practice, can also have beneficial effects on the brain and on the body, and it's certainly our hope that this scientific research will help to convince a wider audience of the importance of this kind of regular practice. Is there anything that you can recommend to us, Your Holiness, that can help people to incorporate this so that it becomes a regular part of their weekly routine, as physical exercise is today? So that we can envision a time in the near future when mental exercise is practiced in the same way that physical exercise is today?

Dalai Lama: That's difficult to say, but one thing is quite sure. I think we must—and some people are already working on this—put further research into how to introduce these secular ethics into the modern educational system. Last year I was in Canada, in Montréal, and I met with about four hundred students representing teacher-training schools across the province of Quebec. The main theme of the meeting was, how can teachers learn to think about ethical education without religion?

Thupten Jinpa: This is partly as a result of a mandate from the Quebec education board, which replaced traditional religious teaching with a new course called Ethics and World Religious Culture.

Dalai Lama: I feel that's very important now. More research is needed on how to introduce secular ethics into the modern educational system, starting from kindergarten and continuing through university. I think the new material that these experts here bring from experience and observation of reality will be important to include in that curriculum. Then people will see the value of these things. Meanwhile, scientists like you should continue research work. The problem is that practitioners' participation in the research has been very limited. So far it's mainly Matthieu.

When I have met on occasion with some Hindu practitioners, some yogis, I told them that the time has come to share some of their experiences, such as inner heat. They can remain in the snowy mountain for months and months without warm clothes, so there must be inner heat. This is not just about individual ambition for fame, but for showing other people the real effects of meditation and yoga practice. It's not just Buddhists who do this, but people in other traditions as well. I heard there are some deep meditation practices in the Christian tradition, and that in some areas of Greece, they still practice traditional Christian meditation. But unfortunately, non-Christians are not allowed, and in some cases, women are not allowed. So we both have no opportunity to go there.

Joan Halifax: That will change, I'm sure. I want to turn to John Dunne. John, your talk about Buddhist economics was integral to understanding universal, or complete, economics. In light of what we've been discussing this morning, we'd appreciate a summary.

John Dunne: Thank you, Joan. I don't know that I have very much to add, Your Holiness, so I'm looking forward to your closing comments. I will say that I am quite encouraged by what I've heard here. There are many reasons to be very hopeful. We've heard that altruism seems to be a fundamental potential within humans. And we know, of course, that in the Buddhist context, there are techniques for cultivating it that seem to be effective. There's even experimental evidence for the possibility that these techniques could be secularized and brought to a wider audience.

Yesterday during the question-and-answer period, some very interesting topics came up. I wanted to point to a couple of those topics in the spirit of challenges. One is the notion that, in terms of our internal economics, we are confused about the causes of happiness. Buddhism poses a challenge to us culturally in the West about that confusion. It comes perhaps best in the form of a Tibetan phrase—*dö chung chôg shé*,[4] or "having few desires and being easily satisfied." In other words, part of the problem for us, culturally, is that we lead lives of distraction, and we are involved so deeply in our external economics that we don't have time to observe our internal economics. Another way of translating that phrase is, "Buy less."

This may not be appropriate for a conference on economics, but here's another challenge that's come up repeatedly, Your Holiness, a very important challenge to us culturally. I think there's a consensus now within the humanities, in several domains, that our notion of self, our notion of identity, has changed over the last several hundred years. We used to have a more interdependent notion of self. We can go back several hundred years to the great Christian mystic and saint Meister Eckhart, who summarized this in a way by saying, "I pray to God that I may not believe in God." In other words, there was an admission, a recognition, that clinging to one's notion of the absolute, clinging to one's notion of identity, was an obstacle to the understanding of interconnectedness and interdependence that is so crucial to the cultivation of altruism.

We've gone through a long period in the West where we've become more atomized, more individualistic. Part of the cultural challenge for us is to use Buddhist wisdom to cut through some of those conceptions of self, and our cultural habits around those conceptions of self, so that our true interconnectedness can more readily flourish. I'm hopeful that we can develop some kind of research agenda, some type of project, that will bring us all forward in this way. I'm very optimistic.

Joan Halifax: Your Holiness, we hope you'll make some concluding remarks.

Dalai Lama: I don't know what to say; I think all the points have already been made. Each session here and really all of the Mind and Life meetings—now, in the last few years, happening almost annually—have been very, very encouraging. There is a clear indication, at least among the participants, that we are not content with the existing state of affairs.

We face many unnecessary problems of our own creation. Certainly nobody wants problems, but we ourselves are often the source of our own problems. Why? First, there is ignorance. Ignorance here means the lack of a holistic way of seeing and understanding. Second, we forget to pay enough attention to inner values. So we human beings have become like slaves to money, slaves to machines. Many intelligent people are now starting to question that kind of existence, asking, what is wrong here? What are some ways to lessen these problems? I think that's a very positive indication. Human development, human evolution, has always occurred in that way. So I think that's very, very encouraging. I myself have learned a lot, but unfortunately, everything I learn during the sessions is forgotten afterward! (*laughter*) So that's bad. Otherwise, this meeting has been wonderful. I hope that the audience has also gotten some new ideas and new views.

To take it further, you can have further discussion and exploration in your own family or among your friends. Contact people, write articles, and when there's a possibility to talk on television, have more discussions about these things. People who lead a miserable life sometimes have no knowledge about how to overcome it, so I think these discussions eventually should be made more public. Then more and more people will show an interest in inner values. For some of them at least, their mental stress may be reduced. Reducing stress, helping people be happier, that's our contribution. That's our goal.

Sooner or later, we have to go and say good-bye to this world. Who will go first among those of us seated here, I don't know, but I think our contribution to this field will benefit generations to come. Thank you.

Notes

Introduction

1. To learn more about the Mind and Life Institute, please visit www.mind andlife.org.
2. See chapters 6 and 10.
3. See chapter 7.
4. See chapters 8 and 11.
5. See chapter 8.
6. Kasser, Tim. 2003. *The High Price of Materialism*. Cambridge: MIT Press.
7. Smith, Adam. (1776) 2008. *The Wealth of Nations*. New York: Oxford University Press, book 1, chapter 2.
8. Edgeworth, F. Y. (1881) 1967. *Mathematical psychics, an essay on the application of mathematics to the moral sciences*. Reprints of Economic Classics. New York: Augustus M. Kelley Publishers, 16.
9. See chapters 3 and 5.
10. See chapter 14.
11. See chapter 9.
12. See chapter 1.
13. See chapters 6 and 10.
14. Stiglitz, Joseph E. 2012. *The Price of Inequality: How Today's Divided Society Endangers Our Future*. New York: W. W. Norton & Company.
15. See chapter 8.
16. Learn more about Mind and Life's publications and research initiatives on page 211.

Notes

Chapter 1

1. La Rochefoucauld, F., Duke de. 1691. *Moral maxims and reflections, in four parts*. London: Gillyflower, Sare & Everingham, maxim 82.
2. Mandeville, Bernard. 1732. *The fable of the bees: or, private vices, public benefits*. London: J. Tonson, 42.

Chapter 2

1. As noted in the introduction, this chapter represents somewhat of a departure from Tania's original presentations in Zurich. Tania made two separate presentations at the event, which are here combined into a single chapter. Tania has continued the research that she presented at the conference; she has updated the chapter text and graphics to represent newer and more accurate data. Despite these changes, the themes and dialogues contained in the chapter still faithfully represent the discussions that took place in Zurich.
2. Lamm, C., J. Decety, and T. Singer. 2011. "Meta-analytic Evidence for Common and Distinct Neural Networks Associated with Directly Experienced Pain and Empathy for Pain." *NeuroImage* 54 (3): 2492–2502.
3. See chapter 3.
4. See chapter 6.

Chapter 3

1. The four *brahmavihāras* are virtues found in Buddhist doctrine: loving-kindness or benevolence; compassion; sympathetic joy; and equanimity.

Chapter 5

1. This incident occurred in August 1996 at the Brookfield Zoo in Brookfield, Illinois. The gorilla was named Binti Jua. A similar event occurred in 1986 between a young boy and a gorilla named Jambo at the Jersey Zoo.

Chapter 6

1. Stigler, George J. 1981. "Economics or Ethics?" In *Tanner Lectures on Human Values,* vol. 2, edited by Sterling McMurrin. Cambridge: Cambridge University Press.
2. Williamson, Oliver E. 1985. *The Economic Institutions of Capitalism.* New York: Free Press, 47.

Chapter 7

1. Wylie: *kun slong.*
2. Wylie: *gzhan phan gyi kun slong.*
3. Wylie: *spyod 'jug.*
4. Sanskrit: *yadā mama pareṣāṃ ca tulyam eva sukham priyam / tadātmanaḥ ko viśeṣo yenātraiva sukhodyamaḥ.* Śāntideva. 1960. "Bodhicaryāvatāra of Śāntideva with the Commentary Pañjikā of Prajñākaramati." In *Buddhist Sanskrit Texts* no. 12, edited by P. L. Vaidya. Darbhanga: The Mithila Institute of Post-Graduate Studies and Research, chapter 8, verse 95.
5. Wylie: *ma gyur sems can thams cad.*
6. Sanskrit: *ye kecid duḥkhitā loke sarve te svasukhecchayā / ye kecit sukhitā loke sarve te 'nyasukheccahyā.* Ibid, chapter 9, verse 129.
7. Wylie: *'phags pa'i nor bdun.*
8. Heim, Maria. 2004. *Theories of the Gift in South Asia.* London: Routledge.
9. Rotman, Andy. 2008. *Thus Have I Seen: Visualizing Faith in Early Indian Buddhism.* New York: Oxford University Press.
10. Wylie: *sbyin pa gtong ba.*

Chapter 10

1. Herrmann, Benedikt, Christian Thöni, and Simon Gächter. 2008. "Antisocial Punishment Across Societies." *Science* 319 (5868): 1362–1367. doi:10.1126/science.1153808.

Chapter 12

1. Since the time of the conference, the 7-billion mark has indeed been achieved, although the exact date of the milestone is not known. The U.N. suggests that the world's 7-billionth baby was born on October 31, 2011. BBC News World. 2011. "Population Seven Billion: UN Sets Out Challenges." Accessed 22 May. [2014?] http://www.bbc.co.uk/news/world-15459643.
2. Chaia, Alberto, Tony Goland, and Robert Schiff. 2010. "Counting the World's Unbanked." *McKinsey Quarterly*. Accessed 22 May. [2014?] http://www.mckinseyquarterly.com/Counting_the_worlds_un banked_2552.
3. See figure 11.1.
4. Source: responsAbility.
5. Bourguignon, François, and Christian Morrisson. 2002. "Inequality among World Citizens: 1820–1992." *The American Economic Review* 92 (4): 727–744. http://www.jstor.org/stable/3083279.

Chapter 13

1. The Doon School, an elite boys' boarding school in Dehra Dun, India, was founded in 1935 and boasts among its alumni many political, scholarly, and business elites, most notably former prime minister Rajiv Gandhi. The Panchen Lama is the second highest-ranking official in Tibetan Buddhism after the Dalai Lama.
2. St. Stephen's College was founded in 1881 as a Christian college. Like the Doon School, it is an elite institution that boasts many distinguished alumni.
3. More than 2,500 people died in the northern state of Bihar during the 1965–1967 famine. Jayaprakash Narayan was a well-known activist and political leader who was a native of Bihar.

Conclusion

1. The Vinaya is a set of scriptures that outline the precepts and codes governing the conduct of monastic members.

Notes

2. Wylie: *ma gyur sems can tham cad*.
3. His Holiness is referring to the great Buddhist university Nalanda, which was located in Bihar, India, and flourished on and off from the fifth to the twelfth century CE.
4. Wylie: *'dod chung chog shes*.

Acknowledgments

The editors would like to thank the many people who helped to make the conference and this book a reality.

First, we wish to thank His Holiness the Dalai Lama for his relentless support, encouragement, and guidance, and for many days of dedicated engagement in Mind and Life. His wisdom, compassion, and teachings are a constant inspiration to us throughout our work and lives.

A deep bow of gratitude also goes to all the speakers and panelists for their wisdom, kindness, and generosity, and the many days of preparation they devoted to the conference and this book. Our thanks also go to the many friends who helped create the conference program by sharing their ideas and contacts, particularly Nina Cenja and Anne Rüffer. Another special thank-you goes to Thupten Jinpa, whose extraordinary skill and dedication as a translator cannot be overstated.

We offer deep thanks to Diego Hangartner for his patience and guidance in bringing this book to life, and for his inspired leadership of the many exciting initiatives being undertaken through Mind and Life Europe.

Many people have contributed to the creation of this book. We thank Zara Houshmand and Kate Beddall for their excellent editorial work during the first phases of the project. Developmental editor Janna White worked with dedication and deftness to bring this book into its final form. Her thoughtful engagement with the material, active partnerships with the authors, and research and writing for the introduction were essential and greatly appreciated.

Inspiration for the introduction was drawn in part from conversations with Richard Layard and Bunker Roy; we thank them for their valuable insights. Lewis Davis and Andy Rotman offered insightful feedback on the introduction. John Dunne rendered the Tibetan phrases to be understandable to all readers.

We are grateful to the many partners, participants, and supporters who made the conference possible. We thank the University of Zurich for cosponsoring this first public Mind and Life conference in Europe, and in particular the Laboratory for Social and Neural Systems Research created by Ernst Fehr, Klaas Enno Stephan, and Tania Singer for its leadership in the emerging field of neuro-economics and its constant efforts to introduce social preferences and emotions into economic models. We also thank Tania Singer's support staff, who assisted with the development of the conference program and helped the staff of Mind and Life in their work on-site.

We thank Mind and Life's sustaining patrons and Gold and Silver sponsors for their critical financial support of this event. The staff at Mind and Life made the conference possible through their attention to the many, many details. We particularly thank Nina Diller for her professional support and dedicated work in Switzerland.

The authors and editors hope that the wisdom and compassion of all the contributors, and the knowledge and spirit of this book, may be carried out into the world and bring happiness to all.

About the Mind and Life Institute

The Mind and Life Institute was cofounded in 1987 by His Holiness the Dalai Lama, the late neuroscientist Francisco Varela, and entrepreneur Adam Engle for the purpose of creating open dialogue and research collaboration between modern sciences, the world's living contemplative traditions, philosophy, humanities, and social sciences. The Mind and Life Institute is founded on the belief that in order to investigate and know the human mind, an integrated, multidisciplinary research collaboration is the most effective approach. Through such an interdisciplinary partnership, a more complete understanding of the nature of reality will be developed; it will alleviate suffering and promote well-being on the planet.

Over the past twenty-five years, the Mind and Life Institute has become a world leader in cultivating this integrated investigation and has developed research fields that explore the effects of contemplative-based practices on the brain, human biology, and behavior.

The work of the Mind and Life Institute is to expand and deepen the investigation of the mind through rigorous scientific research, dialogues on the nature of mind and human qualities, scholarly and contemplative participation, and ongoing support of scientific investigation and the cultivation of a new generation of researchers.

Mind and Life Europe is an integral part of the global strategy to build and support contemplative science and contemplative studies at an international and interdisciplinary level. Established in 2008 in response to increased interest from individuals and institutions, Mind and Life Europe assesses needs, implements strategies, and facilitates programs to help advance the study of consciousness and contemplative practices across Europe. Mind and Life Europe held its first public dialogue in April 2010; this book recounts that inaugural event.

Programs and Initiatives

The Mind and Life Institute seeks to bridge and integrate contemplative wisdom and practices with modern research capabilities and use the resulting knowledge to initiate and catalyze programs to alleviate suffering and support human flourishing around the world. The Institute sponsors numerous programs that support those goals:

- *Dialogues with His Holiness the Dalai Lama*
  Over the years, Mind and Life has organized more than twenty-five private and public events with His Holiness the Dalai Lama in India, the United States, and Europe. The best-known meetings are the biannual private meetings with the Dalai Lama in Dharamsala, which began in 1987. Since 2003, Mind and Life has also hosted public meetings. To view past and upcoming meetings, please visit www.mindandlife.org/dialogues/.

- *Publications*

  Twelve proceedings of meetings with the Dalai Lama have been published as books, including this volume. These include *Train Your Mind, Change Your Brain* by Sharon Begley (Ballantine Books, 2007); *Destructive Emotions* by Daniel Goleman (Bantam Doubleday, 2002); and *The Mind's Own Physician* by Jon Kabat-Zinn and Richard Davidson (New Harbinger Publications, 2012). For a complete list of Mind and Life publications, please visit www.mindandlife.org/publications/.

- *Summer Research Institute*

  Since 2004, the Mind and Life Summer Research Institute (MLSRI) has been held annually at the Garrison Institute in Garrison, New York. The long-term objective of MLSRI is to advance the training of a new generation of developmental scientists, cognitive/affective neuroscientists, applied/clinical researchers, and contemplative scholar/practitioners. Mind and Life Europe will hold the first European Summer Research Institute in 2014. For more information, please visit www.mind andlife.org/sri/.

- *Research Grant Programs*

  The Mind and Life Institute has several grant programs to support ongoing work in the field of contemplative science, including the Varela Awards, the 1440 Awards, and the Contemplative Studies Fellowship. The awards have facilitated more than eighty pilot and novel research initiatives that would otherwise not have been possible, and that have proven to be catalytic to substantial follow-up grants by traditional funding agencies. Learn more at www.mindandlife.org/grants/.

- *Symposium for Contemplative Studies*
  The Mind and Life Institute and Mind and Life Europe both hold a biannual Symposium for Contemplative Studies. These symposia bring together scholars for presentations, discussions, and collaborative networking in the emerging field of contemplative studies, which includes neuroscience, clinical science, contemplative philosophy and the humanities, contemplative education, economics, and those domains of contemplative practice that relate to and interact with these fields of research and scholarship. More information about the next Symposium for Contemplative Studies can be found at www.interna tionalsymposium.org (U.S.) and www.europeansymposium.org (Europe).

The Future of Mind and Life

Mind and Life is entering a new phase of research and development that will focus on application and communication. Some of the major areas for new research initiatives will include Mapping the Mind; Craving, Desire, and Addiction; and Secular Ethics, based on a call from His Holiness the Dalai Lama to promote education in secular ethics around the globe. The goal of all of these initiatives is to promote human flourishing.

In addition to supporting these research initiatives, Mind and Life will take on the task of systematically communicating the outcomes and insights gained through such interdisciplinary research so that they can be accessed and applied by anyone.

List of Contributors

***Tenzin Gyatso, the* 14th Dalai Lama**, is the leader of Tibetan Buddhism and a spiritual leader revered worldwide. Winner of the Nobel Peace Prize in 1989, he is universally respected as a spokesman for the compassionate and peaceful resolution of human conflict. Less well known is his intense personal interest in the sciences: he is a cofounder of the Mind and Life Institute and has said that if he were not a monk, he would have liked to be an engineer. He has a vigorous interest in learning the newest developments in science, and brings to bear both a voice for the humanistic implications of the findings and a high degree of methodological sophistication.

Daniel Batson, PhD, an experimental social psychologist, is a professor emeritus at the University of Kansas and the author of *Altruism in Humans* (Oxford University Press, 2011). His research focuses on the existence of altruistic motivation, the behavioral consequences of religion, and the nature of moral emotions.

Richard Davidson, PhD, is a professor of psychology and psychiatry, director of the Waisman Laboratory for Brain Imaging and Behavior, and founder and chair of the Center for Investigating Healthy Minds at the University of Wisconsin–Madison. A member of the

Mind and Life Institute's board of directors since 1991, he has pioneered the scientific study of how contemplative practice affects the brain.

John Dunne, **PhD**, is an associate professor in the Department of Religion at Emory University, where he is cofounder of the Emory Collaborative for Contemplative Studies. His work focuses on various aspects of Buddhist philosophy, cognitive science, and contemplative practice, and he frequently serves as a translator for Tibetan scholars.

Ernst Fehr, **PhD**, is a professor of microeconomics and experimental economics and chairman of the Department of Economics at the University of Zurich. His research combines insights from economics, social psychology, sociology, biology, and neuroscience to shed light on sociological and psychological aspects of modern economics.

William George, **MBA**, is a professor of management practice at Harvard Business School, where he teaches leadership development and ethics. He is the former chairman and CEO of Medtronic. Under his leadership, the company's market capitalization grew from $1.1 billion to $60 billion, averaging a 35 percent increase each year.

Roshi Joan Halifax, **PhD**, is a Buddhist teacher, Zen priest, anthropologist, and author. She is founder, co-abbot, and head teacher at the Upaya Zen Center, a Buddhist monastery in Santa Fe, New Mexico. Her work focuses on engaged and applied Buddhism, particularly the contemplative care of the dying.

Diego Hangartner, **PharmD**, completed his studies in pharmacology at the Swiss Federal Institute of Technology, where he researched psychoactive drugs and their effects on the mind. After encountering Buddhist methodologies of investigating the mind, he spent eleven years in Dharamsala, India, learning Tibetan, serving as a translator, and leading science workshops for monks. From 2009 to 2012 Diego was the chief operating officer of the Mind and Life Institute. Currently he serves as the director of Mind and Life Europe.

William Harbaugh, **PhD**, is a professor of economics at the University of Oregon who studies why people make charitable donations. In his research, Bill uses methods ranging from economic theory to fMRI neuroimaging to show that the "warm-glow motive" is a powerful incentive to giving.

Antoinette Hunziker-Ebneter, **MB**, is CEO and founding partner of Forma Futura Invest Inc., an independent asset management company focusing on investment opportunities that incorporate good governance and social and environmental responsibility. Earlier in her career, she headed the Swiss stock exchange and was chief executive officer of Virt-x, the first pan-European stock exchange.

Thupten Jinpa, **PhD**, was educated in the classical Tibetan monastic system and received the highest academic degree of Geshe Lharam (equivalent to a doctorate in divinity). Jinpa also holds a BA in philosophy and a PhD in religious studies from the University of Cambridge, U.K. Jinpa has been the principal translator to His Holiness the Dalai Lama since 1985. Jinpa is the president of the

Institute of Tibetan Classics and the chair of the Mind and Life Institute's board of directors.

Lord Richard Layard, PhD, is professor emeritus of economics at the London School of Economics. He was founder-director of its Centre for Economic Performance and now heads CEP's Wellbeing Programme. His work on unemployment, childhood, mental health, and well-being has influenced policy in Britain and beyond.

Matthieu Ricard, PhD, is a Buddhist monk at Shechen Monastery in Kathmandu, Nepal. He holds a PhD in cellular genetics from the Pasteur Institute. He studied with eminent Tibetan teachers Kangyur Rinpoche and Dilgo Khyentse Rinpoche, and has served as French interpreter for His Holiness the Dalai Lama since 1989. A prolific writer and photographer, he devotes the proceeds from his books and much of his time to humanitarian projects in Tibet, Nepal, and India.

Sanjit "Bunker" Roy is an Indian educator, social entrepreneur, and activist. He is the founder of the Barefoot College, an informal, alternative educational institution based on the idea that traditional and indigenous knowledge should be applied to solving rural problems. His innovative educational model has now spread to fifty-four other countries.

Gert Scobel, MA, studied theology and philosophy in Frankfurt and at the Graduate Theological Union in Berkeley, California. In 1988 he joined the ARD, the first German public TV and radio broadcaster, as a documentary filmmaker and host of various science and culture programs. His weekly program, *Scobel*, on 3sat, covers themes ranging from science and culture to social issues. He is the author of two children's books and a fact book on wisdom.

Joan Silk, PhD, is a professor at the School of Human Evolution and Social Change at Arizona State University and former chair of the Department of Anthropology at the University of California, Los Angeles. She is interested in how natural selection shapes the evolution of social behavior in nonhuman primates, and the evolutionary roots of capacities that play a crucial role in human societies, such as reconciliation, cooperation, friendship, paternal investment, and pro-social sentiments.

Tania Singer, PhD, has been the director of the Department of Social Neuroscience at the Max Planck Institute for Human Cognitive and Brain Sciences in Leipzig, Germany, since 2010. She investigates the neuronal, hormonal, and developmental foundations of human social cognition, emotion regulation capacities, and the role of motivation and emotion in social decision making. She also studies the effects of mental training and meditation on the brain and subjective and behavioral plasticity. Tania is on the board of the Mind and Life Institute.

Arthur Vayloyan, PhD, held various executive positions at Credit Suisse from 1992 to 2012. He is a former member of the organization's Private Banking Management Committee, and most recently served as head of the Private Banking Switzerland and Global External Asset Managers divisions. He is particularly interested in nanotechnology, innovation, and microfinance.

Illustration Credits

Figure 1.1: Adapted from Batson, C. D., B. Duncan, P. Ackerman, T. Buckley, and K. Birch. 1981. "Is Empathic Emotion a Source of Altruistic Motivation?" *Journal of Personality and Social Psychology* 40: 290–302, table 3.

Figure 2.1: Adapted from Singer, T., and G. Hein. 2012. "Empathy in Humans and Animals: An Integrative Approach." In *The Primate Mind*, edited by F. B. M. de Waal and P. F. Ferrari. Cambridge: Harvard University Press.

Figure 2.2A: Adapted from Lamm, C., J. Decety, and T. Singer. 2011. "Meta-analytic Evidence for Common and Distinct Neural Networks Associated with Directly Experienced Pain and Empathy for Pain." *NeuroImage* 54 (3): 2492–2502.

Figure 2.2B: Adapted from Bernhardt, B. C., and T. Singer. 2012. "The Neural Basis of Empathy." *Annual Review of Neuroscience* 35: 1–23.

Figure 2.3: Adapted from Klimecki, O. M., S. Leiberg, C. Lamm, and T. Singer. 2012. "Functional Neural Plasticity and Associated Changes in Positive Affect after Compassion Training." *Cerebral Cortex*. Advanced Online Publication. doi:10.1093/cercor/bhs142.

Figures 3.1 and 3.2: Lutz, A., J. A. Brefczynski-Lewis, T. Johnstone, and R. J. Davidson. 2008. "Regulation of the Neural Circuitry of Emotion by Compassion Meditation: Effects of Meditative Expertise." *PLoS ONE* 3 (3): e1897. doi:10.1371/journal.pone.0001897.

Figure 5.2: Silk, J. B. 2008. "Social Preferences in Primates." In *Neuroeconomics: Decision Making and the Brain*, edited by P. Glimcher, C. Camerer, E. Fehr, and R. Poldrack. London: Elsevier, 267–282. Image by Ruby Boyd.

Figure 6.2: Naef, Michael, Ernst Fehr, Urs Fischbacher, Schupp Jürgen, and Gert Wagner, unpublished data. *Decomposing Trust: Explaining National and Ethnic Trust Differences.*

Figure 8.1: Layard, Richard. 2011. *Happiness: Lessons from a New Science*, 2nd ed. London: Penguin, 281–2.

Figure 8.2: Gallup Daily Poll

Figure 8.3: Diener, E., and E. M. Suh, eds. 2000. *Culture and Subjective Well-Being*. Cambridge: MIT Press, 168.

Figure 8.4: Wilkinson, R., and K. Pickett. 2009. *The Spirit Level: Why More Equal Societies Almost Always Do Better*. London: Allen Lane/Penguin, 52.

Figure 9.1: Harbaugh, William, Ulrich Mayr, and Daniel Burghart. 2007. "Neural Responses to Taxation and Voluntary Giving Reveal Motives for Charitable Donations." *Science* 316: 1622. doi:10.1126/science.1140738.

Figure 10.1: Fehr, Ernst, and Simon Gächter. 2000. "Cooperation and Punishment in Public Goods Experiments." *American Economic Review* 90 (4): 980–94.

Figure 11.1: Forma Futura Invest Inc.

Figure 11.2: Otto Scharmer

Figure 12.1: World Bank 2008, http://data.worldbank.org/topic/poverty

DR. TANIA SINGER is the director of the Department of Social Neuroscience at the Max Planck Institute for Human Cognitive and Brain Sciences in Leipzig, Germany.

MATTHIEU RICARD is a French Buddhist monk who resides at Schechen Tennyi Dargyeling Monastery in Nepal. He is the son of the late Jean-François Revel, a renowned French philosopher. He is the author of many bestselling titles, including *The Monk and the Philosopher* and *The Quantum and the Lotus*.